1000

Micro Churches

Dag Heward-Mills

Parchment House

1000 Micro Churches
Copyright © 2022 Dag Heward-Mills

Published by Parchment House 2022
1st Printing 2022

Find out more about Dag Heward-Mills
Healing Jesus Campaign
Write to: evangelist@daghewardmills.org
Website: www.daghewardmills.org
Facebook: Dag Heward-Mills
Twitter: @EvangelistDag

ISBN: 978-1-64330-514-1

Contents

CHAPTER 1

1000
Micro Churches

Then they that gladly received his word were baptized: and the same day there were added unto them about **THREE THOUSAND SOULS.**

Acts 2:41

Praising God, and having favour with all the people. And **THE LORD ADDED TO THE CHURCH DAILY** such as should be saved.

Acts 2:47

The Bible reveals to us a New Testament church that was filled with thousands of souls. The New Testament church was a mega church. When a church has thousands of souls, it is a mega church. A church, which has up to a hundred members, is a micro church. If you have one thousand micro churches that have a hundred members each, you would have one hundred thousand members. Even if you have five members for each of your one thousand micro churches, you would have a congregation of five thousand members. Five thousand members is definitely a mega church.

The vision of having one thousand micro churches is the outworking of the vision of a mega church.

A mega church is built in many different ways. A mega church may be built by having one huge congregation. But a mega church can also be built by having 1000 micro churches. When you put 1000 micro churches together, it creates a mighty, massive, huge, mega church!

Why You Must Build 1000 Micro Churches

1.   You must build 1000 micro churches because it is your way to build a mega church.

Howbeit many of them which heard the word believed; and the number of the men was about FIVE THOUSAND.

Acts 4:4

If God has put into your heart to build a mega church, always remember that building 1000 micro churches will be the fulfilment of the vision to build a mega church. There are many reasons why a mega church cannot be built by having one large congregation.

Sometimes, the city is too large for people to travel to one location every week or twice in a week. Sometimes, there is too much traffic in the city to allow for one mighty massive gathering. Sometimes, your members will travel and be located in different parts of the country but still belong to you and still see you as their shepherd.

Sometimes, the members are forced to migrate into different countries but want to still belong to the same family. As the church develops, there will be many different kinds of church members with different life timetables. Many of your congregants will not be able to gather at the same time to create one huge congregation. However, if you have 1000 micro churches, they will attend one of the micro church services.

Through 1000 micro churches, you will maintain your congregation and not lose your members.

It is God's will to have a mega church. Almighty God has a mega church. There are millions of people in the body of Christ. God has successfully built a mega church made up of thousands of micro churches all over the world. The average size of a church, in the world, is seventy people. This means that the average church is a micro church. Few churches are able to grow to the point where they have thousands of members in one place. Through the vision of 1000 micro churches, you will become an imitator of God. Through the vision of 1000 micro churches, you will achieve much more for God's kingdom.

2. You must build 1000 micro churches because it is your way of being about your Father's business.

And he said unto them, How is it that ye sought me? wist ye not that I must be about my Father's business?"

Luke 2:49

Our Father's business is the business that has to do with God. God is our Father and He has created all creatures to serve Him.

You can be about your father's business, as against being about the banking business, the export business, the import business, the cashew nut business or the gold mining business. God is happy and impressed when some people want to be about His business, rather than their own business. When you want to

3

build a mega church, it means you want to take God's business to the highest height possible.

3. You must build 1000 micro churches because it is your way of defeating satan at the gates of hell.

And I say also unto thee, That thou art Peter, and upon this rock I will build my church; and the gates of hell shall not prevail against it.

Matthew 16:18

All church buildings are positioned at the gates of hell. The gates of hell are mentioned only once in the entire Bible. The gates of hell are associated with the building of the church. Anyone who involves himself in the building of the church will be working next to the gates of hell itself. At the gates of hell, there will be evil powers, evils spirits and wicked entities going in and out, looking at what you are doing.

Most of the demon powers will be surprised to find you so close to hell itself. Most of the demonic powers will be surprised and perhaps even amused, that you would attempt to actually work on such a difficult and dangerous project. Whenever you start building the church, you are defeating satan and his cohorts right in front of their front gate.

Defeating satan at the gates of hell is different from defeating satan at the gate of your house. Defeating satan at the gates of hell means that you have gone into his territory and put him on the defensive. Satan is constantly on the defensive whenever you are building a church.

In his desperation, he will launch counter attacks to try to get you to stop building at his gate. Your enemy is always weaker when you are fighting in front of his gate. No one wants a fight in front of his gate. It is always much better to fight in front of your enemy's gate. When the fight is in front of your gate you have only one chance to make a mistake. When the fight is in front of your enemy's gate, he has only one chance to make a mistake.

Do not be worried about counter attacks. Most of satan's attacks against church buildings are helpless gasps and death gargles of a loser. Those who attack church builders are clutching at straws, trying to find something to weaken their enemy who is overwhelming them.

4. **You must build 1000 micro churches because it is your way of following Jesus and also destroying the works of the devil at the gates of hell.**

    He that committeth sin is of the devil; for the devil sinneth from the beginning. For this purpose the Son of God was manifested, that he might destroy the works of the devil.

    1 John 3:8

    Why did Jesus come into this world? Why was Jesus manifested? To destroy the works of the devil! If Jesus came to this world to destroy the works of the devil, then you must imitate Him to destroy the works of the devil. To destroy the works of the devil, you must locate the devil. Where can you locate the devil but at his gate?

    Find the gate of the enemy and destroy him right in front of his house. Destroying the enemy in front of his house is destroying the enemy at the gates of hell. Destroying the enemy at the gates of hell is the same as building the church.

    It is time to follow Jesus Christ. You have also come into the world to destroy the works of the devil. You will notice that unless you defeat the enemy and gain control, you will not be able to build the church. When you destroy the works of the devil and silence the voice of the slanderer, the accuser and the opposer and the deceiver, you will have peace and rest all around. When you have gained that peace and rest you will be able to build effectively. Notice the scripture below:

    Behold, a son shall be born to thee, who shall be a man of rest; and I WILL GIVE HIM REST FROM ALL HIS ENEMIES ROUND ABOUT: for his name shall be Solomon, and I WILL GIVE PEACE AND QUIETNESS

UNTO ISRAEL IN HIS DAYS. HE SHALL BUILD AN HOUSE FOR MY NAME; and he shall be my son, and I will be his father; and I will establish the throne of his kingdom over Israel for ever.

1 Chronicles 22:9-10

As you can see, peace and quietness is necessary if you are to build the house of God. It was only because Solomon had peace and rest that he was able to build the house of God.

5.   You must build 1000 micro churches because it is the reason for prosperity in the church.

He shall build an house for my name; and he shall be my son, and I will be his father; and I will establish the throne of his kingdom over Israel for ever. Now, my son, the LORD be with thee; and PROSPER THOU, AND BUILD THE HOUSE OF THE LORD THY GOD, AS HE HATH SAID OF THEE.

1 Chronicles 22:10-11

Prosper thou and build the house of God! What a command! What a declaration! What an instruction! "Prosper thou and build the house of God." As you can see from the scripture above, David told Solomon his son to prosper and build the house of God. The only reason for prosperity is in building the house of God. All the houses we build for ourselves are temporary sand castles. God is raising you up and blessing you so that you build His house. That is the reason for prosperity. That is the reason for your high salary. That is the reason for your amazing job. It is to prosper you so that you build the house of God.

6.   You must build 1000 micro churches because that is the way to seek the Lord.

Now set your heart and your soul to SEEK THE LORD YOUR GOD; ARISE THEREFORE, AND BUILD YE THE SANCTUARY of the LORD God, to bring the ark of the covenant of the LORD, and the holy vessels of God, into the house that is to be built to the name of the LORD.

1 Chronicles 22:19

In this amazing scripture, all the princes of David are told to set their hearts to seek the Lord and therefore to arise and build the house of God. As you can see from this amazing scripture, seeking the Lord, arising and building the sanctuary, are one and the same thing.

You will remember the amazing scripture which is a promise to all that as you seek the kingdom of God, all things will be added to you (Matthew 6:33). However, in the book of Chronicles, we see a further revelation on what it means to seek the Lord.

7. **You must build 1000 micro churches because it is your way to access the blessing of fruitfulness.**

And God said, Let us make man in our image, after our likeness: and let them have dominion over the fish of the sea, and over the fowl of the air, and over the cattle, and over all the earth, and over every creeping thing that creepeth upon the earth. So God created man in his own image, in the image of God created he him; male and female created he them. And GOD BLESSED THEM, and God said unto them, BE FRUITFUL, AND MULTIPLY, AND REPLENISH THE EARTH, and subdue it: and have dominion over the fish of the sea, and over the fowl of the air, and over every living thing that moveth upon the earth.

Genesis 1:26-28

God created you to be fruitful. Fruitfulness is a blessing that was given to Adam and Eve when they were created. Anyone who is fruitful is blessed. Many people work to bear fruit and not really for the money. At a certain level in ministry and work, people do not need money but they want to be fruitful. Do you think the royal family is in need of money? I do not think so! They seek after fruitfulness and fulfilment. That is why fruitfulness is a blessing.

When you are fruitful in God, you will feel blessed. When you are fruitful in the church, a blessing will be working on you and through you.

8. You must build 1000 micro churches because it is your way to build a magnificent church for God.

And David said, Solomon my son is young and tender, and THE HOUSE THAT IS TO BE BUILDED FOR THE LORD must be EXCEEDING MAGNIFICAL, OF FAME AND OF GLORY THROUGHOUT ALL COUNTRIES: I will therefore now make preparation for it. So David prepared abundantly before his death.

1 Chronicles 22:5

As you can see from this scripture, the house of God that is to be built must have these characteristics. It must be exceeding magnifical and full of fame and glory. The only way to achieve the building of a church that is "exceeding magnifical, full of fame and glory" is to build 1000 micro churches.

The only way to build a church in all the countries is to build 1000 micro churches. God has a vision for you. You must not let Him down. You must rise up and believe in your heart that it is possible to build 1000 micro churches.

CHAPTER 2

How One Man Can Turn Into 1000 Micro Churches

A little one shall become a thousand, and a small one a strong nation: I the LORD will hasten it in his time.

Isaiah 60:22

1. You are a seed that can become a huge tree.

Another parable put he forth unto them, saying, The kingdom of heaven is like to a grain of mus-tard seed, which a man took, and sowed in his field: Which indeed is the least of all seeds: but when it is grown, it is the greatest among herbs, and becometh a tree, so that the birds of the air come and lodge in the branches thereof.

Matthew 13:31-32

The kingdom of heaven is based on the principle of a little seed that grows into something much much bigger than the seed. You come out from a little seed that is not even visible to the eye. That little seed has grown into this huge human being that you are today. It seems there is no correlation between whom God calls and what he becomes.

You are the little seed that is going to grow into 1000 micro churches. Have faith in God! Do not look at your current size. God does not do things in proportion to your size. Looking at yourself will not help you. It will only kill your faith. Look at the promises of the word of God. The seed is going to become a mighty tree.

2. Jesus was a seed that became a worldwide church.

Verily, verily, I say unto you, EXCEPT A CORN OF WHEAT FALL INTO THE GROUND and die, it abideth alone: but if it die, it bringeth forth much fruit.

John 12:24

Jesus Christ metamorphosed into millions of churches. Right here we see Jesus giving the principle that a person is actually a seed and a seed has the potential of metamorphosing into something much bigger. A seed can become something big and large. You can abide alone but you are capable of being converted into something much bigger. Today, it is up to you to be a seed that will metamorphose into fruits for the whole earth. It is your turn to be metamorphosed into thousands of churches.

3. Jacob and Esau were to become nations when they were in their mother's womb.

And Isaac intreated the LORD for his wife, because she was barren: and the LORD was intreated of him, and Rebekah his wife conceived. And the children struggled together within her; and she said, If it be so, why am I thus? And she went to enquire of the LORD. AND THE LORD SAID UNTO HER, TWO NATIONS ARE IN THY WOMB, and two manner of people shall be separated from thy bowels; and the one people shall be stronger than the other people; and the elder shall serve the younger.

Genesis 25:21-23

When Rebecca wondered why the twins in her struggled together the Lord said to her, "Two nations are in thy womb and two people will be separated from thy bowels and the one shall be stronger than the other..."

God referred to these twins as two nations. If there are 1000 people present, we can safely and prophetically say that there are 1000 nations present now. No one can be idle when there are 1000 churches and 1000 nations to be birthed.

God sees you as a nation! You can become a nation. Jacob and Esau became great nations. The nation of Israel as we know today came out of Jacob. God was right when He said that Jacob was a nation. Today, Israel is represented in the United Nations as a bona fide nation with several million people in it.

4. Jacob crossed over the Jordan and became two bands.

And Jacob went on his way, and the angels of God met him. And when Jacob saw them, he said, this is God's host: and he called the name of that place Mahanaim. And Jacob sent messengers before him to Esau his brother unto the land of Seir, the country of Edom. And he commanded them, saying, Thus shall ye speak unto my lord Esau; Thy servant Jacob saith thus, I have sojourned with Laban, and stayed there until now: And I have oxen, and asses, flocks, and menservants, and womenservants: and I have sent to tell my lord, that I may find grace in thy sight. And the messengers returned to Jacob, saying, we came to thy brother Esau, and also he cometh to meet thee, and four hundred men with him. Then Jacob was greatly afraid and distressed: and he divided the people that was with him, and the flocks, and herds, and the camels, into two bands; And said, If Esau come to the one company, and smite it, then the other company which is left shall escape. And Jacob said, O God of my father Abraham, and God of my father Isaac, the Lord which saidst unto me, Return unto thy country, and to thy kindred, and I will deal well with thee: I am not worthy of the least of all the mercies, and of all the truth, which thou hast shewed unto thy servant; FOR WITH MY STAFF I PASSED OVER THIS JORDAN; AND NOW I AM BECOME TWO BANDS. Deliver me, I pray thee, from the hand of my brother, from the hand of Esau: for I fear him, lest he will come and smite me, and the mother with the children.

Genesis 32:1-11

If God could turn Jacob into two companies, surely, He can turn you into two companies. Surely, He can turn you into two churches! Surely, He can turn you into 1000 micro churches. Surely, He can turn you into a tree!

Jacob, a young man, crossed over the river Jordan. Jacob lived with his uncle for a few years and crossed back. Jacob became two companies by obeying God. Indeed, God blessed Jacob and he multiplied through marriage and through his children and became two companies. Jacob noticed and remembered that the first time he crossed the Jordan, he just had his staff in his hand.

The words of prophecy about two nations being in a womb was coming to pass. Jacob remembered that he had crossed over the River Jordan with just a staff but had become two companies of human beings, cattle, goats, camels and much wealth. Indeed, it is possible for one man to turn into a number of companies.

I think that Jacob was a man of remembrance, and that is why God chose him. He was a thoughtful man. He was a grateful man! He was a man with a good memory. He was a man who recognized that God had actually blessed him. It is important to see God's blessings when they are happening. Not everyone would have remembered passing over the Jordan with just a staff. Some people would have said, "I have worked hard for fourteen years and I deserve to have even five companies." There are different types of people. I pray that you will be like Jacob who notices the grace, the multiplication and the increase when it happens.

Begin to notice how the crowds have increased. Begin to notice how much easier it is for you to get support for the ministry. Begin to notice little things that God has changed in your life.

Begin to notice how much more capable you are of buying chicken and chips. Begin to notice how much easier it is for you to travel somewhere. Begin to notice how much easier it is for you to give an offering. When you notice these little things, God will give you more of them. I once gave a gift to somebody who did not seem to notice that I had given him something. I decided not to give him anything anymore. I even decided not to give his brother anything because I thought, perhaps the whole family does not notice or need such things.

5. God wanted to turn Moses personally into a great nation.

And the LORD said unto Moses, Go, get thee down; for thy people, which thou broughtest out of the land of Egypt, have corrupted themselves: They have turned aside quickly out of the way which I commanded them: they have made them a molten calf, and have worshipped it, and have sacrificed thereunto, and said, These be thy gods, O Israel, which have brought thee up out of the land of Egypt. And the LORD said unto Moses, I have seen this people, and, behold, it is a stiffnecked people: Now therefore let me alone, that my wrath may wax hot against them, and that I may consume them: AND I WILL MAKE OF THEE A GREAT NATION.

Exodus 32:7-10

God said He would make Moses into a great nation. God sees you, a single individual, as a potential nation. God has no problem in turning you into a nation. He can multiply you and make you into 1000 churches.

6. Adam replenished the earth and filled the whole world with people.

And God blessed them, and God said unto them, Be fruitful, and multiply, and REPLENISH THE EARTH, and subdue it: and have dominion over the fish of the sea, and over the fowl of the air, and over every living thing that moveth upon the earth.

Genesis 1:28

God told Adam to fill the world with people. Adam's great commission was to fill the world with people. Our great commission is to fill the world with churches. If God can take one person and fill the whole world with 7 billion people, I do not think He has a problem with taking you and turning you into 1000 micro churches.

It is time to believe that 1000 micro churches will be released into the world through your life and ministry.

7. Noah replenished the earth and filled the whole world with people.

And God blessed Noah and his sons, and said unto them, be fruitful, and multiply, and REPLENISH THE EARTH.

Genesis 9:1

Noah had a great commission as well. His charge was to refill the earth with people. God does not seem to need a group of people to replenish the earth. He gives this amazing and incredulous great commission to replenish the earth to just one man.

I believe that God is doing the same to you today. He is giving you this amazing commission, "Build me 1000 churches!" It is possible to be the pastor of 1000 micro churches. If God could use Noah to fill the whole earth with people, then do not be surprised that He is sending you to do the same.

CHAPTER 3

Become a Leader of 1000 Micro Churches

And THEY WERE SCATTERED, BECAUSE THERE IS NO SHEPHERD: and they became meat to all the beasts of the field, when they were scattered. My sheep wandered through all the mountains, and upon every high hill: yea, my flock was scattered upon all the face of the earth, and none did search or seek after them.

Ezekiel 34:5-6

Y ou must become a leader of one of the one thousand micro churches because it is the fulfilment of the great commission in your life! You must become a leader of one of the one thousand micro churches because you need to bring a lot of people spiritually and physically back into the kingdom of God!

You must become a leader of one of the one thousand micro churches because people have become "meat" for false pastors and you must save them!

You must become a leader of one of the one thousand micro churches because a lot people are lost and you must rescue them! You must become a leader of one of the one thousand micro churches because you are most likely called into the ministry!

Make this declaration over your life right now:

I will become one of the leaders of the 1000 micro churches!

I am becoming one of the leaders of the 1000 micro churches!

I must become a pastor!

I am needed!

I have something to offer!

People are waiting for me to appear!

I cannot let them down!

In the name of Jesus, I surrender all!

1000 micro is for me and I am for the 1000 micro churches!

I will become a church!

Seven Reasons Why You Must Become a Leader of 1000 Micro Churches

1. **You must become a leader of one of the 1000 micro churches because it is a natural stage in the development of your Christian life.**

   For when for the time ye ought to be teachers, ye have need that one teach you again which be the first principles of the oracles of God; and are become such as have need of milk, and not of strong meat.

   Hebrews 5:12

2. **You must become a leader of one of the 1000 micro churches because people are aimless and useless without you. People will be scattered without you entering the ministry.**

   But when he saw the multitudes, he was moved with compassion on them, because they fainted, and were scattered abroad, as sheep having no shepherd.

   Matthew 9:36

3. **You must become a leader of one of the 1000 micro churches so that you gain a good degree in spiritual things.**

   For they that have used the office of a deacon well purchase to themselves a good degree, and great boldness in the faith which is in Christ Jesus.

   1 Timothy 3:13

4. **You must become a leader of one of the 1000 micro churches because the combination of spiritual prosperity with material prosperity is great gain.**

   But godliness with contentment is great gain.

   1 Timothy 6:6

5. **You must become a leader of one of the 1000 micro churches because people are hungry and you need to feed them with the Word.**

And the word of the LORD came unto me, saying, Son of man, prophesy against the shepherds of Israel, prophesy, and say unto them, Thus saith the Lord GOD unto the shepherds; WOE BE TO THE SHEPHERDS OF ISRAEL THAT DO FEED THEMSELVES! should not the shepherds feed the flocks? Ye eat the fat, and ye clothe you with the wool, ye kill them that are fed: but ye feed not the flock. The diseased have ye not strengthened, neither have ye healed that which was sick, neither have ye bound up that which was broken, neither have ye brought again that which was driven away, neither have ye sought that which was lost; but with force and with cruelty have ye ruled them.

Ezekiel 34:1-4

6. **You must become a leader of one of the 1000 micro churches because a lot of people are waiting for you to visit them.**

Therefore thus saith the LORD God of Israel against the pastors that feed my people; Ye have scattered my flock, and driven them away, AND HAVE NOT VISITED THEM: behold, I will visit upon you the evil of your doings, saith the LORD.

Jeremiah 23:2

7. **You must become a leader of one of the 1000 micro churches because you need to strengthen many people.**

And the word of the Lord came unto me, saying, Son of man, prophesy against the shepherds of Israel, prophesy, and say unto them, Thus saith the Lord God unto the shepherds; Woe be to the shepherds of Israel that do feed themselves! should not the shepherds feed the flocks? Ye eat the fat, and ye clothe you with the wool, ye kill them that are fed: but ye feed not the flock. THE DISEASED HAVE YE NOT STRENGTHENED, neither have ye healed that which was sick, neither have ye bound up that which was broken, neither have ye brought again that which was driven away, neither have ye sought that which was lost; but with force and with cruelty have ye ruled them.

Ezekiel 34:1-4

CHAPTER 4

The Assembly and 1000 Micro Churches

Not forsaking the assembling of ourselves together, as the manner of some is; but exhorting one another: and so much the more, as ye see the day approaching.

Hebrews 10:25

Building 1000 micro churches is building a thousand assemblies of God's people. Indeed, our strength is very different when we are together. There is nothing we cannot do if we stay together.

I therefore, the prisoner of the Lord, beseech you that ye walk worthy of the vocation wherewith ye are called, With all lowliness and meekness, with longsuffering, forbearing one another in love; Endeavouring to keep the unity of the Spirit in the bond of peace.

Ephesians 4:1-3

God is the Creator of unity and united existence. God knows the power that comes when we assemble and when we stay together. Indeed, satan saw the effect when God took away the unity from the men of Babel. The confusion that ensued when men spoke different languages and did not understand themselves imparted a profound weakness in men.

And the Lord came down to see the city and the tower, which the children of men builded. And the Lord said, Behold, the people is one, and they have all one language; and this they begin to do: and now nothing will be restrained from them, which they have imagined to do. Go to, let us go down, and there confound their language, that they may not understand one another's speech. So the Lord scattered them abroad from thence upon the face of all the earth: and they left off to build the city.

Genesis 11:5-8

Today, men flounder in desperation and weakness because of disunity and separation. Some men live in affluence whilst most live in abject poverty and difficulty. The problems of many people could be solved just by communicating with someone else. But it is indeed difficult for men to communicate and to understand each other. This difficulty in assembling and doing anything together results in an ultimate deficiency on all mankind.

Through Christ, God is uniting us. He is assembling us together and blessing us with the blessings of the assembly. There are many blessings that come upon us through the assembling of ourselves together. It's time to see that one of satan's ultimate aims is to prevent the saints from assembling.

The more we assemble the better for us. The longer we assemble the better. Have you noticed that there is a lot of criticism when we stay in church for a long time? But there is no criticism for how many hours people stay at parties and watch movies and series of movies? What good do people get out of such things? And so the world, which is led by the "god of this world", discourages the assembly of the saints but encourages every other frivolous, vexatious and immoral activity.

CHAPTER 5

Why the Devil is Against the Assembly

Wherefore we would have come unto you, even I Paul, once and again; but SATAN HINDERED US.

1 Thessalonians 2:18

1. The devil does not like assemblies because it causes the presence of God to be there.

For where two or three are gathered together in my name, there am I in the midst of them.

Matthew 18:20

The presence of God is something the devil hates. Even though God is everywhere and there are Christians everywhere, the promise of "I will be where two or three are gathered in my name" implies a far greater experience of the presence of God in the assembly. The presence of the Lord is in the assembly.

In the name of our Lord Jesus Christ, WHEN YE ARE GATHERED TOGETHER, AND MY SPIRIT, WITH THE POWER OF OUR LORD JESUS CHRIST, To deliver such an one unto Satan for the destruction of the flesh, that the spirit may be saved in the day of the Lord Jesus.

1 Corinthians 5:4-5

You will notice throughout scripture that the power of God does not appear everywhere. Paul asked the Corinthians to gather and experience the power of His presence so that powerful spiritual happenings could take place. The declarations of power could only be made when the gathering of the people took place.

When we gather, His power is present. There are moments when there is a manifestation of the anointing. There are moments when healings take place. And at that special moment special things happen. These are special moments that can only take place in the assembly.

And when they had prayed, the place was shaken where they were assembled together; and they were all filled with the Holy Ghost, and they spake the word of God with boldness.

Acts 4:31

25

You will notice that shaking took place when they were assembled. It is less likely that you would experience shaking, trembling, shivering and other manifestations of the Spirit when you are alone. These things happen in the assembly.

2. The deceptions of the devil are exposed and crowded out in the assembly.

And the great dragon was cast out, that old serpent, called the Devil, and Satan, which deceiveth the whole world: he was cast out into the earth, and his angels were cast out with him.

Revelation 12:9

The presence of other like-minded people who have escaped the deceptions of the devil is one of the blessings in the assembly.

The devil's main work in the world is to deceive. Deception is one of the greatest works of the devil today. To be deceived is to be sent on a journey of destruction. Do you want to be on a journey of destruction? Can you imagine what the world is going to say when they find out that satan has blinded their eyes to the true God and led them calmly into hell fire? They are going to curse satan for all eternity for deceiving them so wildly.

In the assembly of saints, there is reassurance that you are not being deceived. You will see other like-minded people who believe the same things as you. You become reassured that the world is deceived and that you are not deceived through your beliefs in God.

When you meet other like-minded persons, "Iron sharpens iron" (Proverbs 27:11 NIV) and you are encouraged in the truth.

3. The voice of the devil is silenced and lowered in the assembly.

There are, it may be, so many kinds of voices in the world, and none of them is without signification.

1 Corinthians 14:10

There are many voices in the world. Each voice you hear has an effect on you. That is why you must actually block certain voices and not even hear what they have to offer. Jesus said, "Take heed to what you hear..." (Luke 8:18). This is because each voice does have an effect on you. Satan's voice is silenced in the assembly.

Years ago, a young lady was going through a tough time in her marriage. She was at the point of breaking up her marriage. This young lady had been my special daughter for many years and had been a part of the church for many years too. When I called her to try to intervene in the marriage, she refused to talk to me at all. Indeed, she sent me a text stating clearly that she would not be able to speak with me at all and that I should understand her position.

She completely wiped out my voice from her life and her marriage ended. Years later, I mused over her stance and concluded that the devil, did not want her to hear my voice at all. Satan wanted to be the only voice that spoke to that lady.

In the assembly, you will have the voice of God booming out to you. Satan obviously wants people to stay away from the assembly so that his voice is the loudest and only voice listened to.

4. The tricks of the devil are exposed in the assembly.

Put on the whole armour of God, that ye may be able to stand against the wiles of the devil.

Ephesians 6:11

The most dangerous work of the devil for us today is deception. Satan is into tricks and deceptions. You must be ready to overcome works of darkness against you in the form of tricks and deceptions.

Recently, I was speaking to an older man of God. He told me of a crisis he went through in his life and ministry. I was amazed because I was experiencing the exact same crises. He said to me "This is just a passing wind!" I understood many things as he spoke and I became greatly encouraged. It's always a blessing to know that others have been through similar things. It strengthens your resolve to fight on and defeat the enemy.

Without the assembly, you will never know what others have been through. You will never know what God can do. You will never know what God is going to do.

5. The devil is rebuked directly in the assembly.

And they went into Capernaum; and straightway on the sabbath day he entered into the synagogue, and taught. And they were astonished at his doctrine: for he taught them as one that had authority, and not as the scribes. And there was in their synagogue a man with an unclean spirit; and he cried out, Saying, Let us alone; what have we to do with thee, thou Jesus of Nazareth? art thou come to destroy us? I know thee who thou art, the Holy One of God. And Jesus rebuked him, saying, Hold thy peace, and come out of him.

Mark 1:21-25

Jesus dealt with the devil directly in the assembly of the saints. One day, the demon in the man in the synagogue shouted out, "Leave us alone." Actually, the demon could not endure the anti-satanic teachings that were coming forth from Jesus. Demons in you are dealt with directly in the assembly. Do you want to be free from evil spirits? Then come closer and deeper into fellowship with God.

A church does not only need to do special deliverance services in order to deal with demons. Indeed, just the preaching of the word in the assembly is dealing with devils and demons! That is why churches that simply preach and teach the Word also grow larger and larger even if they do not pray for deliverance every week. The Word is a sword and it cuts through the demonic presence with a painful sharpness!

6. The works of the devil are destroyed in the assembly.

He that committeth sin is of the devil; for the devil sinneth from the beginning. For this purpose the Son of God was manifested, that he might destroy the works of the devil.

1 John 3:8

Satan scatters people into the wilderness and Jesus gathers people into an assembly. Every time you gather people, you are destroying the works of the devil. As Jesus lived to assemble and gather people, He was naturally and effortlessly destroying the works of the devil!

The devils aim is to isolate you and take you away from God. Our aim as shepherds is to gather you and bring you closer to God in the assembly. Simply put, we are against satan and we are here to destroy all the works of the devil including the work of scattering people. The assembly exists to destroy the works of the devil.

The good shepherd comes to assemble the scattered people. Jesus was a good Shepherd. He wanted to gather the sheep who were scattered far and wide.

But when he saw the multitudes, he was moved with compassion on them, because they fainted, and were scattered abroad, as sheep having no shepherd. Then saith he unto his disciples, the harvest truly is plenteous, but the labourers are few; Pray ye therefore the Lord of the harvest, that he will send forth labourers into his harvest.

Matthew 9:36-38

A good shepherd sees the need for even more shepherds. He realizes the desperate need of the sheep to be gathered into an assembly. The gathering of the assembly alone will destroy the works of the devil.

7. The devil hates the assembling because he has no meat to eat when they are assembled.

And they were scattered, because there is no shepherd: and they became meat to all the beasts of the field, when they were scattered.

Ezekiel 34:5

Satan wants to chew people up and consume them in his wickedness. If you ever fall into the hands of satan, he will eat you up. Your protection from this wicked beast who seeks to have you for breakfast, is to be a part of the assembly.

It was the lack of assembling that made the sheep prey for the wild beasts. Wild animals in the jungle survive by staying together. Even monkeys and antelopes move together in groups and help each other by the power of the assembly. Buffaloes move along in large herds for protection. Buffaloes are big and strong but are often eaten by lions.

How is a lion able to eat an animal as big as a Buffalo? By isolating one of these huge animals, the lions are able to bring them to the ground and eat them. You will never be eaten by a lion!

Don't forget that assembling is a basic part of Christianity. There are basics like prayer, Bible reading, fellowshipping and honouring fathers that you must never violate. Decide never to violate this basic principle of assembling no matter what is happening in your life.

They go from strength to strength, every one of them in Zion appeareth before God.

Psalm 84:7

Satan is against the assembly because it prevents you from being isolated. Once you are in church you are protected by the presence of the others. It is a natural protection that comes from the assembly.

8. Assembling brings healing to all sicknesses and problems.

And it came to pass on a certain day, as he was teaching, that there were Pharisees and doctors of the law sitting by, which were come out of every town of Galilee, and Judaea, and Jerusalem: and THE POWER OF THE LORD WAS PRESENT TO HEAL THEM.

Luke 5:17

Notice that Jesus did not just experience the power of healing anywhere and anytime. This scripture reveals that the anointing for healing was present at a point when they were assembled.

There must be the assembling of people because it causes the power of God to be present for healing.

Healing is a mysterious ministry that takes place when we assemble. The power of God is a mysterious element that we need to learn to cooperate with and to flow with.

Although healings can take place anywhere and at any time, the assembly causes the power to be manifested even more.

9. Assembling causes the many whom satan has misled, to be saved.

The diseased have ye not strengthened, neither have ye healed that which was sick, neither have ye bound up that which was broken, neither have ye brought again that which was driven away, neither have ye sought that which was lost; but with force and with cruelty have ye ruled them.

Ezekiel 34:4

The assembly leads to the salvation of many people. People get saved when they are in the assembly. Why is that? Salvation becomes possible through the power of the Holy Spirit.

No one can change another human being. It is only by the power of God that true salvation can take place. This is the power that is available in the assembly.

Then they that gladly received his word were baptized: and the same day there were added unto them about three thousand souls.

Acts 2:41

On the day of Pentecost, the large crowd assembled to hear Peter preaching. The assembling of the people released the power of the Spirit for salvation.

10. The assembling causes the satanic starvation of the sheep to end.

Son of man, prophesy against the shepherds of Israel, prophesy, and say unto them, Thus saith the Lord God unto the shepherds; Woe be to the shepherds of Israel that do feed themselves! should not the shepherds feed the flocks? Ye eat the fat, and ye clothe you with the wool, ye kill them that are fed: but ye feed not the flock. The diseased have ye not strengthened, neither have ye healed that which was sick, neither have ye bound up that which was broken, neither have ye brought again that which was driven away, neither have ye sought that which was lost; but with force and with cruelty have ye ruled them. And they were scattered, because there is no shepherd: and they became meat to all the beasts of the field, when they were scattered.

Ezekiel 34:2-5

A good shepherd gathers and assembles the sheep so that he can feed them. Feeding sheep to make them strong is one of the prime goals of the assembly. Satan hates this idea of assembling because he knows it will end the starvation of the sheep. Satan loves to see the people weak and helpless from starvation. The starved and weakened sheep of the pasture are much easier prey for the devil.

Anytime satan sees a feeder arising to give the sheep food he is agitated. Assembling and feeding sheep is a direct assault on satan's kingdom.

The gathering of sheep together will cause them to be fed. Jesus feeds us with the word of God. He gathers and assembles us to feed and be filled.

CHAPTER 6

Powerful Effects of the Assembly

How is it then, brethren? when ye come together, every one of you hath a psalm, hath a doctrine, hath a tongue, hath a revelation, hath an interpretation. Let all things be done unto edifying.

1 Corinthians 14:26

The apostle Paul spends a lot of time explaining how we should behave ourselves in the assembly. He also teaches on what to expect in the assembly. He teaches on what to do "when ye come together".

Indeed the whole of first Corinthians chapter fourteen is about what to do when we come together or when we assemble.

1. The assembly is powerful because it is a place for edification.

For he that speaketh in an unknown tongue speaketh not unto men, but unto God: for no man understandeth him; howbeit in the spirit he speaketh mysteries. But he that prophesieth speaketh unto men TO EDIFICATION, and exhortation, and comfort. He that speaketh in an unknown tongue edifieth himself; but he that prophesieth edifieth the church.

1 Corinthians 14:2-4

Apostle Paul spends the whole of first Corinthians teaching what to do and how to behave in the assembly. He declares that people are expected to be edified in the assembly. One of the greatest effects of the assembly is that you will be edified and built up.

Edification is to be built up in a moral sense. It means to be built up in a religious sense. To be edified means to have an improvement in the mind, in knowledge, in understanding, in morals and in faith.

To be edified is to charge up your batteries. It is a short-term effect of edification.

2. The assembly is powerful because it is a place for exhortation.

For he that speaketh in an unknown tongue speaketh not unto men, but unto God: for no man understandeth him; howbeit in the spirit he speaketh mysteries. But he that prophesieth speaketh unto men to edification, AND EXHORTATION, and comfort.

1 Corinthians 14:2-3

The word "exhortation" comes from the Greek word "*paraklesis*". This word has many beautiful meanings.

An exhortation is a stirring address given by someone. To exhort people means you must do the following:

a. Exert influence upon the will and decisions of another with the object of guiding him into a generally accepted code of behaviour or of entreating him to observe certain instructions.

b. Encourage somebody who is under pressure.

c. Call someone aside for the purpose of strengthening.

d. Put confidence in the troops.

e. To strengthen the morale of the troops by a recollection of past battles. Rehearsing or telling about past victories brings tremendous encouragement.

f. To speak good words so as to encourage or cheer them.

g. To enliven them

h. To reassure them

3. The assembly is powerful because it comforts people.

For he that speaketh in an unknown tongue speaketh not unto men, but unto God: for no man understandeth him; howbeit in the spirit he speaketh mysteries. But he that prophesieth speaketh unto men to edification, and exhortation, AND COMFORT.

1 Corinthians 14:2-3

During the assembly you will have a chance to receive comfort and joy. The Greek word translated into comfort is the word "*paramuthia*".

36

Paramuthia means to speak to another person and to come close to the side of another.

During the assembly, God comes to your side and speaks gently to you, comforting you greatly.

Paramuthia also means to watch over someone by keeping close to the person. Sometimes comfort is administered by just staying close by someone who is grieving. Even without saying anything, comfort is ministered to people. Great comfort is ministered to people who are in the assembly. *Paramuthia* is to speak to someone in a friendly way and to inspire them to courage.

4. The assembly is powerful because it encourages unity.

And the multitude of them that believed were of one heart and of one soul: neither said any of them that ought of the things which he possessed was his own; BUT THEY HAD ALL THINGS COMMON. And with great power gave the apostles witness of the resurrection of the Lord Jesus: and great grace was upon them all.

Acts 4:32-33

And they, continuing daily with one accord in the temple, and breaking bread from house to house, DID EAT THEIR MEAT WITH GLADNESS AND SINGLENESS OF HEART, Praising God, and having favour with all the people. And the Lord added to the church daily such as should be saved.

Acts 2:46-47

The more you meet with somebody, the more united you are with the person. So, the more we come together, the more we become united in the way we think and in the way we do things. Union gives rise to unity. Union is the physical assembling, but unity is the oneness of hearts.

So, coming together (union) gives rise to unity. The more we come together, the more united we become!

5.   The assembly is powerful because it prevents you from turning into a mocker.

How that they told you there should be MOCKERS in the last time, who should walk after their own ungodly lusts. THESE BE THEY WHO SEPARATE THEMSELVES, sensual, having not the Spirit.

Jude 1:18-19

It is mockers and disloyal people who break up the unity of the brethren.   How do people become mockers and disloyal? People turn into mockers by separating themselves.

Those who become mockers are those who separate themselves.

When you separate yourself, you do not have the Holy Spirit. You have a different spirit.

You must be worried when some people do not come to certain meetings. Once you are separated from the assembly, you begin to think in a different way and can easily become a mocker.

People who mock me are usually far from me. They are usually separated and isolated before they become mocking disloyal people.

6.   The assembly is powerful because it causes all needs to be met.

And with great power gave the apostles witness of the resurrection of the Lord Jesus: and great grace was upon them all. Neither was there any among them that lacked: for as many as were pos-sessors of lands or houses sold them, and brought the prices of the things that were sold,

Acts 4:33-34

The church is a place where needs are met. By the assembly, we are able to meet the needs of many people. There are ways your needs can be met. Sometimes your needs can be met through your job, your parents or a relative. But the church and the assembly is another source for your needs to be met.

As you can see from the scripture all the needs of the people were met through the assembly. When I look back on many years of church life, I can see that God has indeed supplied many of my needs through the church.

Have faith in the assembly. You will be surprised that the church will become a source of supply beyond your wildest imaginations. Everything you need, from material to emotional to marital to family needs and wants will be met directly or indirectly through the assembly.

Do not be blind or foolish in not seeing the role of the assembly in providing all the needs of your life. It is wild, mad and immature men who separate themselves from the assembly which is going to provide for them. Perhaps foolish men cannot see far and realize that many needs are indirectly provided for by the assembly.

7. The assembly is powerful because revelation and knowledge are imparted.

Now, brethren, if I come unto you speaking with tongues, what shall I profit you, except I shall speak to you either by revelation, or by knowledge, or by prophesying, or by doctrine?

1 Corinthians 14:6

The apostle Paul spends a lot of time explaining how we should behave ourselves in the assembly, he also teaches on what to expect in the assembly. He teaches on what to do "when ye come together".

How is it then, brethren? when ye come together, every one of you hath a psalm, hath a doctrine, hath a tongue, hath a revelation, hath an interpretation. Let all things be done unto edifying.

1 Corinthians 14:26

A revelation is a striking disclosure of something. It is in the assembly that many revelations are delivered.

To have a revelation is to disclose the realities about a thing and to lay bare the truth.

To have a revelation is to enjoy things which have been hidden and buried out of view.

A revelation is a burst of divine understanding and knowledge.

You can have many revelations in the assembly.

This is because the Spirit is present where two or three are gathered.

God enlightens the people in an assembly. I have received many revelations while preaching. There are times I would start out not fully understanding the message I was preaching and then break out into bursts of revelation as I was speaking.

Trust the Holy Spirit to reveal things to you in the assembly. The assembly is a powerful place to be. When God tells you to preach about something, simply obey Him and the revelations will flow. The revelations will flow even more in the assembly.

One afternoon I was playing golf and I heard the Spirit say, "Preach about sacrifice this evening." At that time, I had never preached on that topic before. That evening I was amazed at the revelations that flowed from me. In the assembly, the Holy Spirit moves mightily and powerfully.

You can also expect to receive knowledge in the assembly. Knowledge brings understanding and causes you to enter into a truth and grasp it.

Knowledge is what distinguishes people on earth. The world is divided into the "haves" and the "have nots". But even more significantly it is divided into "those who know" and "those who don't know".

Those who know how to make and export cars, planes, phones, televisions, computers, watches, bicycles and such like are separated by a great gulf from those who do not know how to do anything of the sort.

In the assembly, you will receive a great revelation and abundance of knowledge which will separate you greatly from those who do not come to the assembly and consequently know nothing!

8. The assembly is powerful because prophecy will happen there.

So likewise ye, except ye utter by the tongue words easy to be understood, how shall it be known what is spoken? for ye shall speak into the air....

If therefore the whole church be come together into one place, and all speak with tongues, and there come in those that are unlearned, or unbelievers, will they not say that ye are mad? But if all prophesy, and there come in one that believeth not, or one unlearned, he is convinced of all, he is judged of all: And thus are the secrets of his heart made manifest; and so falling down on his face he will worship God, and report that God is in you of a truth. How is it then, brethren? when ye come together, every one of you hath a psalm, hath a doctrine, hath a tongue, hath a revelation, hath an interpretation. Let all things be done unto edifying.

1 Corinthians 14:9, 23-26

a. A prophecy is discourse emanating from divine inspiration.

b. A prophecy will declare the mind of God in any given situation.

c. A prophecy speaks as the voice of God.

d. A prophecy speaks with authority.

e. A prophecy speaks as an oracle.

Indeed, it is in the assembly that you sense the inexplicable authority of God's voice thundering down at you. God is present in the assembly. God will respond to the assembling of His saints by speaking clearly to us all.

9. The assembly is powerful because doctrines are released.

How is it then, brethren? when ye come together, every one of you hath a psalm, HATH A DOCTRINE, hath a tongue, hath a revelation, hath an interpretation. Let all things be done unto edifying.

1 Corinthians 14:26

A doctrine is a pattern and a series of teachings with a characteristic style. God wants to give patterns of teachings to help the church to remember the messages. God is a good God and He releases doctrines to create a movement. Every doctrine is the basis of a movement.

When you teach in series and in patterns it creates a movement. Repetitive teachings and continuous preaching about the same things create a pattern and the pattern in turn creates a movement.

Indeed, repeated teachings about the Holy Spirit created the Pentecostal Movement.

Repeated teachings about the gifts of the Spirit created the Charismatic Movement.

Repeated teachings in a methodical way created the Methodist Movement.

In the assembly, you will find the place to repeatedly teach on what God has given you. You will soon be the leader of a brand-new move of God.

Doctrines are gradual, systematic, fundamental ways of teaching that are imparted in stages. Doctrines will establish the instructions and teachings as a way of thinking and living.

This is why we preach in series. There must be a trend and pattern of thinking. People take a long time to learn things; that is why we preach in series and also preach the same things over and over again.

10. Assembling is powerful because prayer is released.

And being let go, they went to their own company, and reported all that the chief priests and elders had said unto them. And when they heard that, they lifted up their voice to God with one accord, and said, Lord, thou art God, which hast made heaven, and earth, and the sea, and all that in them is:

Acts 4:23-24

It is much easier to pray in the assembly than all alone. This is because when you are alone you only hear yourself praying and the monotony of it dulls you to sleep.

In the assembly there is always another person who is more zealous than you. In the assembly, there is always another person who can pray louder and more excitedly than yourself. As he wanes in his prayer, another person picks up and the chain goes on. I find myself praying more zealously for many hours when I am in an assembly.

God wants you to use the advantage of the assembly to improve your prayer life greatly.

Prayers that will shake the place will be released in the assembly.

CHAPTER 7

Transformation and 1000 Micro Churches

Do not conform to the pattern of this world, but BE TRANSFORMED by the renewing of your mind. Then you will be able to test and approve what God's will is—his good, pleasing and perfect will.

Romans 12:2 (NIV)

Key No.1 - TRANSFORMATIONAL POWER:

I beseech you therefore, brethren, by the mercies of God, that ye present your bodies a living sacrifice, holy, acceptable unto God, which is your reasonable service. And be not conformed to this world: but be ye transformed by the renewing of your mind, that ye may prove what is that good, and acceptable, and perfect, will of God.

Romans 12:1-2

Yes, you can be transformed into a pastor of one of the 1000 micro churches. Indeed, you can also be a man of God who gives birth to a 1000 micro churches. What an amazing privilege.

So how can I be transformed from an ordinary person into someone so significant in the kingdom of God? Decide not to be conformed to the world! Don't join the rat race but be transformed! To be transformed, you must take the big step of NOT BEING CONFORMED to the world around you.

Before any kind of transformation occurs, you must be determined not to be the same as everybody else. Do not be conformed to the world.

The people in our world are looking for money, wealth, position and power. Every one around you is chasing something!

To experience this transformational power, you must not join the rat race of life.

How do you not join the rat race of life? By analysing everything the world is doing and seeing the futility in most of the things men are chasing. It takes great wisdom to see the futility of the activities of men. Solomon was a man of great wisdom and he saw the futility of life and work on this planet. He said many times that all that man was engaged in was futile. Be not conformed to the world means that you will not follow the futility that the world is following.

> I have seen all the works that are done under the sun; and, behold, all is vanity and vexation of spirit.
>
> Ecclesiastes 1:14

Solomon went as far as to hate life and to hate work on earth. Why did Solomon feel this way? Because he was a wise man with a little more wisdom than the rest of the people on earth who had joined the rat race of futile ventures. Solomon was not conformed to this world.

> Therefore I hated life; because the work that is wrought under the sun is grievous unto me: for all is vanity and vexation of spirit. Yea, I hated all my labour which I had taken under the sun: because I should leave it unto the man that shall be after me.
>
> Ecclesiastes 2:17-18

Instead of setting your life's goals to be things you will never get and to spend all your energy on things that will never satisfy, you will now focus on God and His kingdom.

This switch in focus will transform your life radically and make you a totally different human being.

Key No.2 - METAMORPHOSIS POWER:

You will be transformed into the pastor of 1000 micro churches through the metamorphosis power of the Holy Spirit.

> Now the Lord is that Spirit: and where the Spirit of the Lord is, there is liberty. But we all, with open face beholding as in a glass the glory of the Lord, are changed into the same image from glory to glory, even as by the Spirit of the Lord.
>
> 2 Corinthians 3:17-18

Today you are in need of being changed from a fruitless and barren Christian ministry to a fruitful and flourishing tree of righteousness. How can that happen? How does that work? Through metamorphosis power!

There is indeed another power that changes you from glory to glory. It is called metamorphosis power. We are changed from glory to glory by the Spirit of the Lord through this metamorphosis power.

This kind of change is radical and extreme in its nature. That is the kind of change that occurs when a caterpillar is changed into a butterfly. Think about it! A caterpillar is ugly and stuck to the ground. A butterfly is pretty and free to fly around like a bird. What a metamorphosis! Only God can effect such a major change in your life.

There are two major keys needed to deploy metamorphosis power. The first is an open face! An open face speaks of openness and availability. Being open to God's servant is key to receiving the power that will release metamorphosis power into your life. This is why satan is on a campaign of slander to pour calumny and slime on all of God's servants and to blacken their reputation as much as possible. The more a minister of God looks or appears evil, the less open you will be to receive anything from him.

The second key to metamorphosis power is to behold the glory as in a glass. The more you look at glory the more you will change into what you are looking at. Keep looking at good things you can admire. Do not spend your time looking at the mistakes of a man of God. You will soon find yourself making the same mistakes that you accuse somebody of. You will change into the same thing. That's why it is dangerous to look at evil things like pornography. You will find yourself changing into what you see.

That's why I watch videos of men of God that I admire. As I keep watching the crusades and conferences on video I am changing into the exact same image. Don't watch evil films that denigrate and malign God's servants. God wants to release metamorphosis power into your life through the beholding of glory!

Key No.3 - WORD POWER:

O how love I thy law! it is my meditation all the day. Thou through thy commandments hast made me wiser than mine enemies: for they are ever with me. I have more understanding than all my teachers: for thy testimonies are my meditation. I understand more than the ancients, because I keep thy precepts. I have refrained my feet from every evil way, that I might keep thy word.

Psalm 119:97-101

How will someone like you be made into a great man of God? Through WORD POWER! How will you be transformed into a pastor of 1000 micro churches? Through Word power!

You can be transformed by the Word power of God. You will be transformed by the word of God into many amazing things.

1. By loving the law of God and meditating on it constantly, you will be changed into something wonderful.

2. You will become someone who is wiser than all your enemies through the word of God.

3. You will be changed into someone wiser than even teachers, by the power of the word of God.

4. You will become like an ancient wise man through the power in the word of God.

What a transformation that comes into your life through the word of God - becoming so wise, wiser than enemies and even teachers just because of the word of God.

You must give yourself to listening to the word of God all the time. You must read and read the word of God. You must watch videos about the word of God.

The word of God is a changing metamorphosing force in the world today.

Key No.4 - ANOINTING POWER:

Then Samuel took a vial of oil, and poured it upon his head, and kissed him, and said, Is it not because the Lord hath anointed thee to be captain over his inheritance? When thou art departed from me to day, then thou shalt find two men by Rachel's sepulchre in the border of Benjamin at Zelzah; and they will say unto thee, The asses which thou wentest to seek are found: and, lo, thy father hath left the care of the asses, and sorroweth for you, saying, What shall I do for my son? Then shalt thou go on forward from thence, and thou shalt come to the plain of Tabor, and there shall meet thee three men going up to God to Bethel, one carrying three kids, and another carrying three loaves of bread, and another carrying a bottle of wine: And they will salute thee, and give thee two loaves of bread; which thou shalt receive of their hands. After that thou shalt come to the hill of God, where is the garrison of the Philistines: and it shall come to pass, when thou art come thither to the city, that thou shalt meet a company of prophets coming down from the high place with a psaltery, and a tabret, and a pipe, and a harp, before them; and they shall prophesy: AND THE SPIRIT OF THE LORD WILL COME UPON THEE, AND THOU SHALT PROPHESY WITH THEM, AND SHALT BE TURNED INTO ANOTHER MAN.

1 Samuel 10:1-6

The anointing will turn you into a pastor of 1000 micro churches. Perhaps there is nothing that you need more than the Holy Spirit and the anointing. Saul was turned into another man because of the anointing that came over him. I have written many books on the anointing because I believe it is the one supernatural thing that you must seek above all others. Do whatever you can to become anointed.

Elisha was asked an amazing question by Elijah. "What do you want from me?" Elisha gave the best answer that any clever person could ever give. He said; "I want the anointing on your life and I want double!"" (2 Kings 2:9) Indeed, he got it and the wisdom of his reply is there for all to see.

Choose the anointing above all else!

By opening yourself to the anointing of the Holy Spirit and desiring it so much and asking for it above all else, you will receive a changing and transformative power in your life through the anointing.

Key No.5 - THE DOERS' POWER - IMPLEMENTATION POWER:

BUT BE YE DOERS OF THE WORD, and not hearers only, deceiving your own selves. For if any be a hearer of the word, and not a doer, he is like unto a man beholding his natural face in a glass: For he beholdeth himself, and goeth his way, and straightway forgetteth what manner of man he was. But whoso looketh into the perfect law of liberty, and continueth therein, he being not a forgetful hearer, but a doer of the work, this man shall be blessed in his deed.

James 1:22-25

Do something. There is no way you can be transformed into a micro church pastor without doing something practical. Implementing the word of God and instructions you have received will turn you into a pastor of one thousand micro churches.

Be a doer of something.

Doing something, no matter how small, is the key to the doers' power. Doers of the Word do small things which become big things.

And so he that had received five talents came and brought other five talents, saying, Lord, thou deliveredst unto me five talents: behold, I have gained beside them five talents more. His lord said unto him, Well done, thou good and faithful servant: thou hast been faithful over a few things, I will make thee ruler over many things: enter thou into the joy of thy lord. He also that had received two talents came and said, Lord, thou deliveredst unto me two talents: behold, I have gained two other talents beside them. His lord said unto him, Well done, good and faithful servant; thou hast been faithful over a few things, I will make thee ruler over many things: enter thou into the joy of thy lord.

Matthew 25:20-23

Most people are discouraged by the smallness of their gift. Do not let that deter you anymore. No matter how small and insignificant you are just DO SOMETHING.

Start now and God will bless your little efforts and make you great. Someone asked me whether he should back out of a ministry opportunity because of a looming crisis. I told him; "This is your Goliath! If you are able to win over this crisis you will be another David who has killed a Goliath."

Don't back down from killing a Goliath when he appears, you may never get another chance to kill a Goliath. That means you may never get other chances to be famous and great in the ministry.

Do something when the opportunity presents itself. Don't back down from your golden opportunities of ministry. Don't worry about the tension and stress you feel. That is part of the ministry and part of the journey to greatness.

Key No.6 - SERVANT POWER:

That it might be fulfilled which was spoken by Esaias the prophet, saying, BEHOLD MY SERVANT, WHOM I HAVE CHOSEN; MY BELOVED, in whom my soul is well pleased: I will put my spirit upon him, and he shall shew judgment to the Gentiles. He shall not strive, nor cry; neither shall any man hear his voice in the streets. A bruised reed shall he not break, and smoking flax shall he

51

not quench, till he send forth judgment unto victory. And in his name shall the Gentiles trust.

Matthew 12:17-21

Being a servant is not the same as becoming inferior. Jesus did not become inferior when He became a servant. Being a servant will make you a pastor of 1000 micro churches. Jesus has demonstrated for all eternity, the path to transformation. Become a servant! Jesus became the King of kings by becoming a servant.

Be a servant like Jesus! Anyone can be a servant! Being a servant is the great step to become like Jesus. Serve in one way or another!

Jesus is the greatest example of someone who changed from a carpenter into the King of kings and Lord of lords. Jesus became the best example of a good shepherd.

Do what He did! Being a servant is being godly. Godliness is to be a servant. Jesus was the Son of God and, also, He was God. Yet He was a servant. That is the greatest endorsement of the ministry of a servant. Being a servant is being godly!

Key No.7 - FAITH POWER:

And Jesus answering saith unto them, Have faith in God. For verily I say unto you, that whosoever shall say unto this mountain, Be thou removed, and be thou cast into the sea; and shall not doubt in his heart, but shall believe that those things which he saith shall come to pass; he shall have whatsoever he saith.

Mark 11:22-23

Faith power will change everything. The power of faith is the power to move a mountain from one location to another. That same power can move you from being a pastor of nobody to becoming the pastor of thousands.

Faith is your life! Faith is the decisions you take! Take the decisions to walk by faith.

Faith is to go forward and build 1000 micro churches. Faith power is released through a small step of obedience

Your faith will be seen from your life.

Faith is to make adjustments and fight to build a mega church.

Faith is to lead with strength, to act with speed and to do anything that is necessary to build 1000 micro churches.

By faith, I predict you will pass your tests that are now before you in this journey to 1000 micro churches.

Faith will make you climb every wall to build the church. No wall will be too high for you! Every river can be crossed by faith! Every river can be crossed by faith! You will cross all the rivers that are before you and hindering you from your goal of 1000 micro churches.

Every mountain in your life can be flattened by faith. Therefore, every mountain that hinders you from becoming a pastor of 1000 micro churches is flattened today in the name of Jesus.

Faith will make you endure affliction. You will be able to go through every affliction that you must go through in order to build 1000 micro churches.

Faith will enable you to abandon wealthy cities for Christ. Faith will enable you to abandon everything you need to abandon so that you can build 1000 micro churches.

Faith giants are created by hearing! You will become a spiritual faith giant by hearing and seeing and meditating on the word of God. When you are a giant, you will have 1000 micro churches as your fruits.

Faith is an unstoppable force! You are an unstoppable force as you press on to build 1000 micro churches.

Faith launches you into the miracle ministry. Through faith power, you will be launched into 1000 micro churches.

Faith is a force that can suspend the laws of nature. The laws of nature may not allow you to become a thousand churches. But through faith power, you will transcend the laws of nature and build 1000 micro churches.

Faith blocks curses and exempts you from evil! You are exempted from every evil attack, as you endeavour to build 1000 micro churches.

Faith moves quickly and does greater works. 1000 micro churches will be the greater works that you will accomplish.

Faith will empower you to subdue nations with 1000 micro churches.

Faith enables you to overcome superior enemies and build 1000 micro churches.

Faith overcomes rejection in the communities that you are sent to.

Faith will turn your weaknesses into strength!

Faith is operating with the consciousness of the invisible powers that are helping you to build 1000 micro churches.

Faith is partnering with the invisible to accomplish the impossible task of building 1000 micro churches.

Faith is a power that converts barrenness to fruitfulness! You will no longer sit alone without several congregations looking up to you for leadership and inspiration.

Faith is the power that converts your failures in ministry into success upon success.

Faith grafts you into the family of mega church pastors today!

Faith forces God's hand to perform wonders and build 1000 micro churches.

Faith is a powerful inexorable creative force that is going to create 1000 micro churches.

Faith loves the adventure of building 1000 micro churches.

Faith says "Yes" to the adventure of building 1000 micro churches.

Faith has an unlimited capacity for visions. That is why you are able to accept the idea of building 1000 micro churches.

Faith is the trigger for the supernatural release of power to build 1000 micro churches.

Faith brings glory into your life. Faith will make you beautiful before God.

Faith is not in a hurry to impress any one. Through the mystery of faith, you will accomplish the impossible for God. (See my book *"Faith Secrets"*)

CHAPTER 8

How to Have 1000 Micro Churches: Preach the Word

PREACH THE WORD; be instant in season, out of season; reprove, rebuke, exhort with all longsuffering and doctrine.

2 Timothy 4:2

Your ministry can change and multiply into 1000 churches. Instead of having one little congregation, you can have 1000 churches. How is that possible? It is possible by preaching the word of God.

Preaching the word of God is the most important duty of a pastor. It is important because it is what gives life and vitality to the sheep. If you become an expert feeder of the sheep, your flocks and herds will multiply and you will have 1000 little congregations, instead of having one little congregation which even struggles to exist.

Some people's churches are like football teams which struggle to stay in the first division. They are always in danger of relegation. Every football season that passes is not a season for them to win any trophy but rather a struggle to prevent relegation to a lower division. Some churches are just struggling to survive the season and be able to declare that they still exist.

So when they had dined, Jesus saith to Simon Peter, Simon, son of Jonas, lovest thou me more than these? He saith unto him, Yea, Lord; thou knowest that I love thee. He saith unto him, Feed my lambs.

John 21:15

Jesus asked Peter for only one thing. Feed my lambs! That is what was important to Jesus - the feeding of the lambs and sheep! It is time to take the feeding, preaching, teaching and counselling of the sheep as seriously as possible. That's all that Jesus wants you to do.

Satan has two plots up his sleeve. The first is to get you to not become a preacher. If that fails, satan's plan is to get you to preach things that are close and parallel to the word of God.

Close and parallel preaching is on topics like secular leadership, secular wisdom, human rights, secular success, social campaigns, politics, health education etc. Unfortunately, preaching messages that are close and parallel to the word of

God do not save souls. Close and parallel messages do not lead to healing and deliverance! Close and parallel teachings give rise to mental pleasures and good feelings. But there is no real accomplishment in Spirit. Sheep do not eat sand! Sheep eat grass. Sand may be close and parallel but it is not grass.

The preaching of the word of God is in preaching on topics like the work of ministry, the word of faith, salvation, baptism of the Holy Spirit, the anointing, faithfulness, Christian character, repentance and love.

What you teach will change the church! You need to have confidence in the word of God. If the Word is indeed the word of God, then it should have supernatural effects on the people it is fed to.

For we are God's fellow workers [His servants working together]; you are God's cultivated field [His garden, His vineyard], God's building.
1 Corinthians 3:9 (AMP)

Why do some places have thick rich forests and others have dry brown plains? It is the amount of rain that falls on a place that determines how the vegetation multiplies. Your church is God's garden. If you water it a lot it will change and grow into a thick forest of 1000 micro churches.

Don't be ashamed of the true word of God. Do not follow cleverly devised fables.

Give the hard truths of the Word to your church and your congregation will become a forest with uncontrollable growth of tall trees and a very thick undergrowth.

CHAPTER 9

Constant Preparation for 1000 Micro Churches

There be four things which are little upon the earth, but they are exceeding wise: The ants are a people not strong, yet they prepare their meat in the summer;

Proverbs 30:24-25

I t is exceedingly wise to be in a state of constant preparation.

You must be in a state of constant preparation so that the word of God will be in your heart. You will never be a good preacher unless your preaching is from your heart. And you will never really preach from your heart unless you are always in a constant state of preparation!

Why is preaching from the heart so important? Because it is only when preaching is from your heart that it impacts the hearers. Jesus clearly taught us that it is things that are done from the heart that have an ability to change or affect us.

And he saith unto them, are ye so without understanding also? Do ye not perceive, that whatsoever thing from without entereth into the man, it cannot defile him; Because it entereth not into his heart, but into the belly, and goeth out into the draught, purging all meats? And he said, That which cometh out of the man, that defileth the man. For from within, out of the heart of men, proceed evil thoughts, adulteries, fornications, murders, thefts, covetousness, wickedness, deceit, lasciviousness, an evil eye, blasphemy, pride, foolishness: All these evil things come from within, and defile the man.

Mark 7:18-23

This is why your heart must be kept with all diligence; because your heart is the place where power and authority springs from. Indeed, Solomon the wise man declared that the heart is the source of the springs of life.

Watch over your heart with all diligence, for from it flow the springs of life.

Proverbs 4:23 (NASB)

The spring of life-giving water that waters and grows God's field into a luscious forest will not come from your mind but your heart. Every man of God who releases life-giving water will see a field full of growing trees. It's time to stop ministering words that just give mental pleasures. It's time to stop using big words and quoting from encyclopaedias just to impress the world.

Get the true Word deep into your heart and minister the word of God as a life-giving force. You will soon see 1000 micro churches, instead of a struggling church trying to prevent relegation!

Constant preparation is needed because of opportunities that will come when you are not expecting them. Be ready for the greatest opportunity of your life by being in constant preparation.

Do not forget the famous formula:

Preparation + Opportunity = Success!

Thousands of hours of preparation are needed for a few hours of preaching. You will need a much longer time of preparation than the actual preaching. Prepare for one hour to preach for five minutes.

Athletes prepare for thousands of hours just to run for ten seconds!

I was once in Jamaica and I saw a famous sprinter training on the tracks. I was amazed at the time and effort he was putting into his training. Someone was running behind him and pulling him back with a kind of belt so he could run and train against pressure. All these hours spent on training were just to win a race that lasts nine seconds!

CHAPTER 10

How to Practice Constant Preparation

But solid food is for the mature, for those who have their powers of discernment trained by CONSTANT PRACTICE to distinguish good from evil.

Hebrews 5:14 (ESV)

1. Constant preparation is by a constant daily quiet time

This book of the law shall not depart out of thy mouth; but thou shalt meditate therein day and night, that thou mayest observe to do according to all that is written therein: for then thou shalt make thy way prosperous, and then thou shalt have good success. (Joshua 1:8)

How can I constantly prepare to preach and teach? By constantly meditating, thinking and brooding on the word of God day and night! You must meditate on the word of God all the time because that is what will be coming out of your mouth very soon.

One of the main secrets to having good success is the pastor's day and night quiet time. Joshua was the new leader of God's people. He was admonished to keep the Word in his heart day and night in order to have good success as a leader.

If you have a church that is struggling to fight off relegation, you are not having good success. Good success will come by God's way. God's way to good success is to study the Bible daily and nightly and to meditate on it all the time so that you start obeying fully.

I wish I could tell you that all pastors have their daily quiet time. Indeed, many pastors tell people to have their quiet time but they themselves do not have a daily or nightly quiet time.

If I was asked what is one of the big secrets of my ministry, I would say it is the daily quiet time I have with God. The quiet time of Bible reading and prayer every single day no matter what is happening is a great secret to success.

Most of the revelations I received have come to me through my daily quiet time. All the books I have written come from this quiet time. A daily quiet time is a kind of constant preparation.

For you to constantly prepare to preach and teach you would need some amazing strategies. You need to have some strategies. It is not natural to meditate on the word of God all the time.

Decide to go through a particular book of the Bible every day. Read a few verses of a chapter and stop at exactly where the Holy Spirit seems to be speaking. Stop at every word or sentence or phrase that strikes you. Then stay there and meditate. Think about it and turn it over in your mind till the full revelation comes to you.

Through the Holy Spirit, many verses of the Bible will become revelations, counsel and supernatural guidance to you every day.

2. Constant preparation is by reading Christian books

And Shaphan the scribe shewed the king, saying, Hilkiah the priest hath delivered me a book. And Shaphan read it before the king. And it came to pass, when the king had heard the words of the book of the law, that he rent his clothes. And the king commanded Hilkiah the priest, and Ahikam the son of Shaphan, and Achbor the son of Michaiah, and Shaphan the scribe, and Asahiah a servant of the king's, saying, Go ye, enquire of the Lord for me, and for the people, and for all Judah, concerning the words of this book that is found: for great is the wrath of the Lord that is kindled against us, because our fathers have not heark-ened unto the words of this book, to do according unto all that which is written concerning us.

2 Kings 22:10-13

Reading books is important for your constant preparation. The life of king Josiah reveals the power of reading in the life of a believer. The reign of king Josiah changed dramatically through reading.

The Bible states that the priest Hilkiah found a "Book of the Law" in the temple during the early stages of Josiah's temple renovation. Hilkiah then gave the scroll to his secretary Shaphan, who took it to King Josiah. According to the Bible, King Josiah then changed his form of leadership entirely, entering into a new form of covenant with the Lord. He wiped out all of the pagan cults that had formed within his land. He, along with his people, then entered into this new covenant with the Lord to keep the commandments of the Lord. What an amazing impact book reading had on Josiah.

Constantly read books and you will constantly experience dramatic changes in your mind heart and soul.

You will never be a good preacher unless you read books constantly. Obviously, Apostle Paul was an avid reader too. We know Apostle Paul was an avid reader from two things. First, because he called for his books and parchments to be brought to him.

And Tychicus have I sent to Ephesus. The cloke that I left at Troas with Carpus, when thou comest, bring with thee, and the books, but especially the parchments.

2 Timothy 4:12-13

We also know Apostle Paul was a reader because of his numerous quotations from other books. Apostle Paul quoted from the first five books of the Old Testament at least 45 times. Then, Apostle Paul quoted from the prophets 53 times.

Apostle Paul quoted from Isaiah alone 36 times. This great apostle also quoted from the Book of Psalms 23 times.

The Quotations of Paul from the Books He Read

1. Apostle Paul quoted from Psalm 14:2-3 in Romans 3:10-12

   Romans 3:10-12 - As it is written, There is none righteous, no, not one: There is none that understandeth, there is none that seeketh after God. They are all gone out of the way, they are together become unprofitable; there is none that doeth good, no, not one.

   Psalm 14:2-3 - The Lord looked down from heaven upon the children of men, to see if there were any that did understand, and seek God. They are all gone aside, they are all together become filthy: there is none that doeth good, no, not one.

2. Apostle Paul quoted from Psalm 5:9 and Psalm 140:3 in Romans 3:13

   Romans 3:13 - Their throat is an open grave; they use their tongues to deceive. The venom of asps is under their lips.

   Psalm 5:9 - For there is no faithfulness in their mouth; their inward part is very wickedness; their throat is an open sepulchre; they flatter with their tongue.

   Psalm 140:3 - They have sharpened their tongues like a serpent; adders' poison is under their lips. Selah.

3. Apostle Paul quoted from Psalm 10:7 in Romans 3:14

   Romans 3:14 - Their mouth is full of curses and bitterness.

   Psalm 10:7 - His mouth is full of cursing and deceit and fraud: under his tongue is mischief and vanity.

4. Apostle Paul quoted from Isaiah 59:7-8 and Psalm 36:1 in Romans 3:15-18

   Romans 3:15-18 (ESV) - "Their feet are swift to shed blood; in their paths are ruin and misery, and the way of peace they have not known." "There is no fear of God before their eyes."

   Isaiah 59:7-8 - Their feet run to evil, and they make haste to shed innocent blood: their thoughts are thoughts of iniquity; wasting and destruction are in their paths. The way of peace they know not; and there is no judgment in their goings: they have made them crooked paths: whosoever goeth therein shall not know peace.

   Psalm 36:1 -The transgression of the wicked saith within my heart, that there is no fear of God before his eyes.

5. Apostle Paul quoted from Genesis 15:6 in Romans 4:3

   Romans 4:3 (NASB) - For what does the Scripture say? "Abraham believed God, and it was counted to him as righteousness."

   Genesis 15:6 - And he believed in the LORD; and he counted it to him for righteousness.

6. Apostle Paul quoted from Psalm 32:1-2 in Romans 4:7-8

   Romans 4:7-8 (ESV) - Blessed are those whose lawless deeds are forgiven, and whose sins are covered; blessed is the man against whom the Lord will not count his sin

   Psalm 32:1-2 - Blessed is he whose transgression is forgiven, whose sin is covered. Blessed is the man unto whom the LORD imputeth not iniquity, and in whose spirit there is no guile.

7. Apostle Paul quoted from Genesis 17:10 in Romans 4:11

   Romans 4:11 (ESV) - He received the sign of circumcision as a seal of the righteousness that he had by faith while he was still uncircumcised. The purpose was to make him the father of all who believe without being circumcised, so that righteousness would be counted to them as well,

   Genesis 17:10 - This is my covenant, which ye shall keep, between me and you and thy seed after thee; Every man child among you shall be circumcised.

8. Apostle Paul quoted from Genesis 17:5 in Romans 4:17

   Romans 4:17 (ESV) - as it is written, "I have made you the father of many nations"—in the presence of the God in whom he believed, who gives life to the dead and calls into existence the things that do not exist.

   Genesis 17:5 - Neither shall thy name any more be called Abram, but thy name shall be Abraham; for a father of many nations have I made thee.

9. Apostle Paul quoted from Genesis 15:5 in Romans 4:18

Romans 4:18 (ESV) - In hope he believed against hope, that he should become the father of many nations, as he had been told, "So shall your offspring be."

Genesis 15:5 - And he brought him forth abroad, and said, Look now toward heaven, and tell the stars, if thou be able to number them: and he said unto him, So shall thy seed be.

10. Apostle Paul quoted from Exodus 20:17 in Romans 7:7

Romans 7:7 (ESV) - What then shall we say? That the law is sin? By no means! Yet if it had not been for the law, I would not have known sin. For I would not have known what it is to covet if the law had not said, "You shall not covet."

Exodus 20:17 - Thou shalt not covet thy neighbour's house, thou shalt not covet thy neigh-bour's wife, nor his manservant, nor his maidservant, nor his ox, nor his ass, nor any thing that is thy neighbour's.

11. Apostle Paul quoted from Psalm 44:22 in Romans 8:36

Romans 8:36 (ESV) – As it is written, "For your sake we are being killed all the day long; we are regarded as sheep to be slaughtered."

Psalm 44:22 - Yea, for thy sake are we killed all the day long; we are counted as sheep for the slaughter.

12. Apostle Paul quoted from Jeremiah 9:24 in 1 Corinthians 1:31

1 Corinthians 1: 31 (NASB) - So that, as it is written, "Let the one who boasts, boast in the Lord."

Jeremiah 9:24 - But let him that glorieth glory in this, that he understandeth and knoweth me, that I am the Lord which exercise lovingkindness, judgment, and righteousness, in the earth: for in these things I delight, saith the Lord.

13. Apostle Paul quoted from Isaiah 64:4 in 1 Corinthians 2:9

1 Corinthians 2:9 (ESV) - But, as it is written, "What no eye has seen, nor ear heard, nor the heart of man imagined, what God has prepared for those who love him."

Isaiah 64:4 - For since the beginning of the world men have not heard, nor perceived by the ear, neither hath the eye seen, O God, beside thee, what he hath prepared for him that waiteth for him.

14. Apostle Paul quoted from Deuteronomy 25:4 in 1 Corinthians 9:9

1 Corinthians 9:9 (ESV) - For it is written in the Law of Moses, "You shall not muzzle an ox when it treads out the grain." Is it for oxen that God is concerned?

Deuteronomy 25:4 - Thou shalt not muzzle the ox when he treadeth out the corn.

15. Apostle Paul quoted from Deuteronomy 27:26 in Galatians 3:10

Galatians 3:10 (ESV) - For all who rely on works of the law are under a curse; for it is written, "Cursed be everyone who does not abide by all things written in the Book of the Law, and do them."

Deuteronomy 27:26 - Cursed be he that confirmeth not all the words of this law to do them. And all the people shall say, Amen.

16. Apostle Paul quoted from Habakkuk 2:4 in Galatians 3:11

Galatians 3:11(ESV) – Now it is evident that no one is justified before God by the law, for "The righteous shall live by faith."

Habakkuk 2:4 - Behold, his soul which is lifted up is not upright in him: but the just shall live by his faith.

17. Apostle Paul quoted from Leviticus 18:5 in Galatians 3:12

Galatians 3:12 - And the law is not of faith: but, The man that doeth them shall live in them.

Leviticus 18:5 - Ye shall therefore keep my statutes, and my judgments: which if a man do, he shall live in them: I am the Lord.

18. Apostle Paul quoted from Deuteronomy 21:23 in Galatians 3:13

Galatians 3:13 - Christ redeemed us from the curse of the law by becoming a curse for us—for it is written, "Cursed is everyone who is hanged on a tree."

Deuteronomy 21:23 - His body shall not remain all night upon the tree, but thou shalt in any wise bury him that day; (for he that is hanged is accursed of God;) that thy land be not defiled, which the LORD thy God giveth thee for an inheritance.

19. Apostle Paul quoted from Deuteronomy 25:4 in 1 Timothy 5:18

1 Timothy 5:18 - For the scripture saith, Thou shalt not muzzle the ox that treadeth out the corn. And, The labourer is worthy of his reward.

Deuteronomy 25:4 - Thou shalt not muzzle the ox when he treadeth out the corn.

20. Apostle Paul quoted from Psalm 68:18 in Ephesians 4:8

Ephesians 4:8 - Wherefore he saith, When he ascended up on high, he led captivity captive, and gave gifts unto men.

Psalm 68:18 - Thou hast ascended on high, thou hast led captivity captive: thou hast received gifts for men; yea, for the rebellious also, that the Lord God might dwell among them.

21. Apostle Paul quoted from Zechariah 8:16 in Ephesians 4:25

Ephesians 4:25 - Wherefore putting away lying, speak every man truth with his neighbour: for we are members one of another.

Zechariah 8:16 - These are the things that ye shall do; Speak ye every man the truth to his neighbour; execute the judgment of truth and peace in your gates:

22. Apostle Paul quoted from Genesis 2:24 in Ephesians 5:31

Ephesians 5:31 (ESV) - "Therefore a man shall leave his father and mother and hold fast to his wife, and the two shall become one flesh."

Genesis 2:24 - Therefore shall a man leave his father and his mother, and shall cleave unto his wife: and they shall be one flesh.

23. Apostle Paul quoted from Exodus 20:12 and Deuteronomy 5:16 in Ephesians 6:2-3

Ephesians 6:2-3 - Honour thy father and mother; (which is the first commandment with promise;) That it may be well with thee, and thou mayest live long on the earth.

Exodus 20:12 - Honour thy father and thy mother: that thy days may be long upon the land which the Lord thy God giveth thee.

Deuteronomy 5:16 - Honour thy father and thy mother, as the LORD thy God hath com-manded thee; that thy days may be prolonged, and that it may go well with thee, in the land which the LORD thy God giveth thee.

24. Apostle Paul quoted from Isaiah 45:23 in Philippians 2:10

Philippians 2:10 - That at the name of Jesus every knee should bow, of things in heaven, and things in earth, and things under the earth;

Isaiah 45:23 - I have sworn by myself, the word is gone out of my mouth in righteousness, and shall not return, That unto me every knee shall bow, every tongue shall swear.

It is clear that Apostle Paul was reading from these books and therefore quoting extensively from what he had read. The Book of Isaiah was a prophetic book that showed how Jews and Gentiles would be forged into one family whilst the Book of Psalms spoke much of Jesus the Messiah. These were certainly books Apostle Paul would have enjoyed and soaked in. Have books everywhere! Have books in every place you ever sit to rest for a few minutes and always take the chance to read something small. That is the key to constant preparation.

3. Constant preparation is by listening to messages

Listening to preaching messages all the time is key to constant preparation. By listening to messages, you open yourself to many advantages. Look at this amazing list of blessings you receive from listening to preaching and teaching:

1. You receive direction and counsel for your life as you soak in preaching and teaching.

2. You stay in the presence of God as you soak in messages. You take church home with you as you keep listening to the word of God.

3. You turn into a minister of the word of God without intending to. Listening to the word of God is the most casual way to turn into a pastor of 1000 micro churches.

4. You fall in love with good preaching as you listen to messages preached. You will never become something you don't admire.

5. You begin to admire and love the person who preaches. It is good to admire and love the preacher and teacher. It is that love for the preacher that opens your spirit to receiving the anointing from a man of God.

6. As you listen to messages from the word of God, you will learn about the different types of messages that exist. Listening more causes you to appreciate the difference between an exhortation and a teaching as well as the difference between an evangelistic message and a pastoral message.

7. You will even learn the different types of anointing that operate in a person. You will notice when a preacher is flowing in the anointing of a prophet or in a teacher's anointing.

8. You will learn how to title a message when you listen to messages. You will learn to give dramatic titles to evangelistic messages and calming but interesting titles to pastoral titles.

9. You will learn how to give exhortations to people to get saved. I learnt how to give exhortations urging people to be saved by watching and listening to Billy Graham and others.

10. You will learn how to preach in series by listening to people preach in series. When you pastor a church, you have to have something to say every week. People are waiting to hear from God every week even though they've been listening to you the whole year. Every good teacher can get 31 teaching messages from one exhorter's message.

11. You will learn the meaning of words when you listen to messages. Every preacher uses words that you don't understand. He will explain the meanings of certain words and you will have great revelation when you read your Bible again.

12. You will learn how to end messages. Many don't know how to end on a happy note. It takes experience to end a service well. People have to feel uplifted even if they have been rebuked.

13. You will learn how to do an altar call by listening to messages. I learnt how to do altar calls by listening to Jimmy Swaggart. I could listen several times over to the five minute altar call he gave in a message. I even tried to learn how to cry as he did, when doing an altar call although I have never managed to cry during an altar call.

14. You will learn how to preach to unresponsive congregations by listening to messages. It is an art to preach to silent people with blank faces. There are messages that will teach you how to do that excellently.

15. You will learn how to preach to different cultures and peoples by listening to messages. God will teach you many things as you listen to messages.

16. You will learn how to preach to huge and heavy crowds by listening to someone doing that. I learnt how to preach to thousands by watching Reinhard Bonnke. I noticed he could speak to half a million people as though he was talking to one little boy!

17. You end up learning and memorizing verses that you hear over and over. You may not have set out to memorize scripture. But you will find out that you are beginning to quote what you keep hearing.

18. You will learn how to give the right number of scriptures for each occasion. Some people preach without quoting the scriptures. A lack of scripture in a message is a mistake of the highest proportions. There must be enough scripture to back every single point you make.

19. You will learn also how not to give too many scriptures in one message. Indeed, there are many scriptures that can buttress one point and a preacher can give too many references in one message.

20. You will learn how to preach to dignitaries by listening to messages. The rich and the poor are different in their

reception and understanding of the word of God. Your aggressive posture alone might offend the dignitaries and they might be put off in the first few minutes of your preaching. Preaching to dignitaries is an art to learn by watching and learning.

21. You will learn to preach to people of other religions by listening to messages. There is a way to stir up hatred and anger when you preach about Jesus but there is also a way to make peoples of other religions desire the love and healing that comes from Jesus Christ.

22. By listening to messages, you will learn how to do different types of altar calls. You will learn how to make altar calls for salvation, for deliverance, for finances, for marriage, for backsliders, for breakthroughs and the work of ministry. There are many things to learn by watching and listening to messages!

4. Constant preparation is by constant investment in preaching

For where your treasure is, there will your heart be also.

Matthew 6:21

Investing in the word of God takes your heart deeper into God. This depth in the word of God is a great form of preparation for your ministry.

Invest in good preaching and teaching. Spend money on the word of God. What you spend money on reveals where your heart is. Some people do not want to spend any money on books and materials. They feel it should be free. The truth is that it is free. But you should see it as a treasure which is worth more than anything else.

When your heart is in the word of God, your ministry will change. I have not yet seen a ministry thrive that does not invest in and treasure visiting preachers. There are times I have visited churches which are more concerned with saving money than honouring the person who has ministered to them. I have ministered in places where the pastor had no respect or acknowledgment for me and my message. They had no honour and no respect for the word. It is rare for such people to ever be honoured themselves.

Many churches closed down after they despised the word of God and the messenger of God. I once ministered to a church out of my heart. The pastor took offense at my message and rebuked me sharply for my message. Indeed, my message was seen as an interference! The next time I heard of him his church building was being sold. When you don't treasure the word of God, it does not work for you.

Invest in the message and invest in the messenger! Giving a good honorarium is a way of investing in the treasure of the word. That shows where your heart is.

Buy books, buy videos, buy Bibles and buy gadgets that help you receive the word of God. Buy audio books! Buy listening devices! Invest in the word of God and you will be mightily blessed.

CHAPTER 11

Timothy Principles for 1000 Micro Churches

Thou therefore, my son, be strong in the grace that is in Christ Jesus. And the things that thou hast heard of me among many witnesses, the same commit thou to faithful men, who shall be able to teach others also.

2 Timothy 2:1-2

Timothy Principle 1:   There are some messages that are only for sons and daughters

> Thou therefore, my son, be strong in the grace that is in Christ Jesus.
>
> 2 Timothy 2:1

"Thou therefore my son!" There are messages that are intended for sons. If you are a son, you will hear much more than if you are not a son. Indeed, it is a painful experience to give messages to outsiders who rubbish your beautiful wisdom.

I once preached in two different churches in a large city. One of the churches was extremely happy to receive me and listen to my message. The other church was extremely offended at my message and never wanted to see my face again.

It is indeed a lesson in maturity to know that some people are not worthy of hearing certain things. They must remain in their ignorance and darkness. That is why Jesus preached to the Pharisees in parables. He didn't want to give them light and understanding because they were wicked men.

> He answered and said unto them, Because it is given unto you to know the mysteries of the kingdom of heaven, but to them it is not given... For this people's heart is waxed gross, and their ears are dull of hearing, and their eyes they have closed; lest at any time they should see with their eyes, and hear with their ears, and should understand with their heart, and should be converted, and I should heal them.
>
> Matthew 13:11, 15

Learn to deliberately keep certain people in the dark because of their wickedness and Pharisee like attitudes.

Timothy Principle 2:   You must be strong in the grace that is available in your particular ministry

> Thou therefore, my son, be strong in the grace that is in Christ Jesus.
>
> 2 Timothy 2:1

It is not every church that has grace in a certain area. Grace means help, assistance in a certain area. Be strong in the grace that is there. There is a grace that is available for me and my ministry. I intend to walk in that grace fully. I am enjoying the grace for teaching, church growth and church planting. Be stronger in what you are already strong in!

I once heard that the Chinese ping-pong coaches said that they do nothing about their weaknesses, they only strengthen their strengths. Amazing! Strengthen what you are strong in! Be strong in the grace! This principle of developing their strengths has made them world champions in ping-pong.

Perhaps, you have a special grace to teach women. Perhaps you have a special grace for the healing anointing. Become stronger in that grace. I must be an outstanding teacher because that is the grace on me. If you are under my ministry, you must seek out the graces that are here and get stronger in them.

Timothy Principle 3: Your ministry is a product of what you hear

> And the things that thou hast heard of me among many witnesses, the same commit thou to faithful men, who shall be able to teach others also.
>
> 2 Timothy 2:2

Your ministry is directly proportional to what you have heard!

Timothy's ministry was a product of what he had heard, the messages he had listened to and the personal counselling he had received from apostle Paul.

Paul said to Timothy "The things that thou hast heard of me commit these to faithful men." Timothy could not have had a ministry if he had not heard many things.

Your ministry is a product of what you have heard from God. Your ministry is a product of what you have heard from other men of God. Your ministry is a product of the messages you have lis-tened to.

Your ministry is directly proportional to the number of messages you have soaked in!

Timothy Principle 4: Preach the same things with the same titles

And the things that thou hast heard of me among many witnesses, the same commit thou to faithful men, who shall be able to teach others also.

2 Timothy 2:2

One day I watched a movie in which someone was being given instructions on what to do on his military mission.

One of the key instructions was "Don't be a hero." In other words, don't try to do anything that would make you stick out and be different. Don't try to make yourself famous by attempting things which will not make much difference any way. Don't try to make a difference which no one needs.

Stay within bounds and let's get out of this mission safely and humbly!

That is the kind of advice Paul was giving to Timothy when he told him to preach the same things. Do not be ashamed of preaching the same things with the same titles.

Paul expected this of Timothy. If you are trying to impress people, you are doing something wrong and it is from a wrong spirit. Rather try to impress God. Do not be ashamed of preaching the same things.

Do not be ashamed to preach the same thing with the same title.

Timothy Principle 5: Raise up pastors and leaders who can also teach

And the things that thou hast heard of me among many witnesses, the same commit thou to faithful men, who shall be able to teach others also.

2 Timothy 2:2

Preach in such a way as to raise up pastors and leaders who will also be able to teach the word of God. Most people preach in such a way as to comfort encourage and soothe the members. It is a good thing to encourage people, but it takes much more than encouragement and comfort to create an army of 1000 micro church leaders. You can have 1000 micro churches if you accept to raise up pastors out of the ordinary congregation members sitting in front of you every Sunday.

You must spend even more time talking to faithful men than just everybody. It's nice and exciting to speak to the large crowds that gather on Sundays. You must now allow yourself to spend even more quality time with the people who are faithful and constant in their obedience and implementation of your words.

The mark of your success as a teacher and a pastor is that you have been able to teach people who have risen up to also become pastors and teachers. Notice that phrase - "who shall be able to teach others also".

Pastors, you are successful when you are producing other pastors and teachers.

This was apostle Paul's secret to 1000 micro churches; produce people who can also teach others.

CHAPTER 12

Sacrifice for 1000 Micro Churches

I beseech you therefore, brethren, by the mercies of God, that ye present your bodies a liv-ing sacrifice, holy, acceptable unto God, which is your reasonable service. And be not con-formed to this world: but be ye transformed by the renewing of your mind, that ye may prove what is that good, and acceptable, and perfect, will of God.

Romans 12:1-2

1. **You have to sacrifice because there is nothing like a convenient ministry.**

It was not convenient for Jesus Christ to come to this world and to die on the cross for us. If you want a convenient ministry, you cannot build 1000 micro churches.

2. **You must sacrifice because sacrifice is a basic and foundational aspect of serving God.**

Sacrifices began with Abel and Cain. Sacrifice continued with Abraham, Isaac and Jacob. These three patriarchs built altars and sacrificed to God. David and Solomon were known to have made great sacrifices for God. Sacrifice is part of building 1000 micro churches. NO SACRIFICE, NO CHURCH!

3. **You must sacrifice in order to gain favour with God.**

In the book of Genesis, we see how Abraham became a friend of God by being willing to sacrifice his only son. (Genesis 22:16, James 2:23)

4. **Sacrifice is the key that will make you fruitful.**

Except the seed fall into the ground and die it abideth alone (John 12:24). The missing ingredient in good, honest, willing, educated, informed Christians is sacrifice. Through sacrifice, educated, knowledgeable, principled Christians will become fruitful.

5. **You must sacrifice because it is an anti-satanic practice to sacrifice.**

When the anti-Christ comes he will stop people from sacrificing to God in the temple. This is the spirit of the anti-Christ. This anti-Christ spirit says, 'Stop the sacrifice!" (Daniel 8:11-13.) Without sacrifice, no missionaries would ever have been sent to Ghana.

6. Sacrifices are redirected into other things by the anti-Christ.

The anti-Christ offered a pig on the Jewish altar. This was an abomination. Apostle Paul said, the things they sacrifice, are sacrificed to devils. The devil seeks to replace God and receive sacrifices that are meant for God.

But I say, that the things which the Gentiles sacrifice, they sacrifice to devils, and not to God: and I would not that ye should have fellowship with devils

1 Corinthians 10:20

Amon was two and twenty years old when he began to reign, and reigned two years in Jerusalem. But he did that which was evil in the sight of the LORD, as did Manasseh his father: FOR AMON SACRIFICED UNTO ALL THE CARVED IMAGES WHICH MANASSEH HIS FATHER HAD MADE, AND SERVED THEM; And humbled not himself before the LORD, as Manasseh his father had humbled himself; but Amon trespassed more and more.

2 Chronicles 33:21-23

7. Sacrifice in order to come nearer to God.

When you start your journey in the Tabernacle towards the Holy of Holies, you first encounter the Altar of Sacrifice. A sacrifice must be made if you want to come near to God. (Hebrews 9:6-7 NKJV)

8. Sacrifice in order to qualify as a minister of the Gospel.

Then Peter began to say unto him, LO, WE HAVE LEFT ALL, AND HAVE FOLLOWED THEE. And Jesus answered and said, Verily I say unto you, There is no man that hath left house, or brethren, or sisters, or father, or mother, or wife, or children, or lands, for my sake, and the gospel's, But he shall receive an hundredfold now in this time, houses, and brethren, and sisters, and mothers, and children, and lands, with persecutions; and in the world to come eternal life.

Mark 10:28-30

In order to come to Jesus, you will have to take up your cross and follow Him. You will have to deny your family, your brothers, your sisters, your wife and your children.

9. Sacrifice in order to be counted as a Christian. A disciple is a follower of Jesus Christ.

And whosoever doth not bear his cross, and come after me, cannot be my disciple.

Luke 14:27

10. Sacrifice in order to take your room in the ministry.

And Jehu the son of Nimshi shalt thou anoint to be king over Israel: and Elisha the son of Shaphat of Abelmeholah shalt thou anoint to be prophet in thy room.

1 Kings 19:16

There is a room that you must occupy in the ministry. You will never take your place among the pastors of 1000 micro churches, unless you pay the price for it.

CHAPTER 13

1000 Micro Churches
and the Art of
Leading Worship

Sing unto him a new song; play skilfully with a loud noise.

Psalm 33:3

You will need to develop the art of leading worship if you want to have 1000 micro churches. Music will always be important in a mega church. 1000 micro churches will grow bigger and faster as you learn and grow in true worship.

How to Lead Worship

1. Be in a state of constant preparation. You will never be a good worship leader if you do not prepare properly.

2. Admire worship leaders. You will never become something you don't admire.

3. Learn the songs of a worship leader that you admire. The songs of a worship leader are his trade mark.

4. Listen to worship and praise music all the time. Just as you listen to preaching messages, you must listen to worship music. As you listen to worship music, you will start to sing the same things in the same way, without even intending to.

5. Shamelessness (*anadeia*) is essential to become a good worship leader. Like with the learning of languages, the ability to sing is greatly enhanced by shamelessness. Do not be intimidated. Use your voice. It will improve!

6. Practice leading worship at home. Practice leading worship at home in front of the mirror. Practice, at least ten times, until you are very sure.

7. Choose a series of songs that can never fail you. Write down the songs. Rehearse them over and over.

8. Learn the interludes and copy them exactly. It is the interludes that mark out and characterize a particular worship leader.

9. Sing from your heart. If you don't feel a certain way about the song you will be too stiff to impart to the people.

10. Soak in the song until it gets into your heart. Then you will be able to sing from your heart. We moved away from hymns because many of them ceased to be sang from the

heart. Some hymns have such beautiful words but people stopped singing them from the heart. Also, some of the hymns were too wordy to be sang from the heart.

11. Use energy in order to maintain the pitch or note. You need energy to maintain a certain note otherwise you will go off all the time. If you come on stage with a spirit of tiredness and laziness the worship will not be nice.

12. Ignore instrumentalists. Do not include them in your plan to become a good worship leader. They will frustrate your plans. You will be the best worship leader if you can sing without instruments. Otherwise you will be very limited in what you can do. In a new church there are often no instrumentalists.

13. Choose your own key and start out on your own.

14. Have a back up singer to help you. Have someone who sings with a back-up microphone. He/she can fill in for you when you are out of breath.

15. Learn how to switch on a microphone. Don't hit the microphone because it destroys it. Many keep singing not even knowing that the microphone is off.

16. Learn how to hold the microphone properly. Some cover their face with the mic and some hold it like a cigarette. Some hold the microphone at waist level! It is important to know how to hold the microphone.

17. Maintain a sweet spirit. Do not be angry when leading worship. Do not show irritation and anger on stage. It is not easy to switch from an angry spirit to a worshipping spirit.

18. Dress properly. In the church, instrumentalists must dress properly. Instrumentalists must not look like street children or ruffians.

19. Lady worship leaders must choose the right length of clothes. A lady worship leader must be exquisite, noble, elegant, decent, respectable, impressive, presentable,

acceptable, professional, beautiful but not lustful and sexual. Lady worship leaders must show a spirit of subjection and submissiveness. It is important to have an attitude of subrather than an attitude of aggression so that the people can receive you.

20. Ladies must have an attitude of subjection and submission. It is important not to appear to be shouting at or putting down the people you are leading.

21. Be confident about your voice. Your voice is one of the good voices. Know that your voice will improve as you lead worship. Your voice and your singing abilities will deteriorate or stay the same if you do not sing at all.

22. Develop the art of teaching songs to the congregation. Take the time to teach the songs and it could be the beginning of a great worship leading career.

23. Lead worship in small groups.

24. Develop appropriate body movements and gestures.

25. Sing with emotion. A good worship leader is someone who shows his feelings. You must be able to lead worship and shed some tears. People who behave like ice blocks will not make good worship leaders.

26. Lady worship leaders must do their hair nicely. All lady worship leaders must have a stand-by wig that they can put on in case they have the need to.

27. Maintain eye contact with the congregation at all times. Your control and ability to lead is dependent on keeping eye contact. You may close your eyes at times but keep your eyes open intermittently so you can see the congregation.

28. Control the congregation. Don't lose the congregation. Stop the song if people are not singing and talk to the congregation to join in.

29. Flow with songs that work.

30. Sing relevant and meaningful songs. If the song you're singing is not relevant it will kill the atmosphere.

31. Catch the anointing to be a worship leader. It is by the anointing that you can lead worship. Being a worship leader is under the office of helps and is a gift from God.

CHAPTER 14

Abide in the Anointing for 1000 Micro Churches

But the fruit of the Spirit is love, joy, peace, forbearance, kindness, goodness, faithfulness, gentleness and self-control. Against such things there is no law.

Galatians 5:22-23 (NIV)

Threa fruits of a longstanding and abiding anointing are love, joy, peace, forbearance, kindness, goodness, faithfulness, gentleness and self-control. You need to abide in the anointing for many years if you are going to build 1000 micro churches. I am writing this chapter to encourage you to stay under the anointing for many years. Allow the Holy Spirit to have a greater effect on your life and personality. The Holy Spirit is the rain from God. The Holy Spirit is God's river flowing through your life. The longer it rains and the longer a river has passed through an area, the greater the change will be. Places without rain and rivers are very different from places with lots of rain.

The Holy Spirit's presence in your life can be a nine-day wonder. The Holy Spirit's presence in your life can also be a longstanding event with many fruits to show for it. The fruits of the Spirit are the fruits of the anointing that have been in place for a long time.

The anointing of the Holy Spirit has many effects. There are short term and long-term effects of the anointing of the Holy Spirit. Most Christians are used to hearing that miracles, healing and such manifestations are the indications of the anointing of the Holy Spirit.

Indeed, they are indications of the anointing of the Holy Spirit. However, as the Holy Spirit lingers, and as the anointing remains, there will be other effects. When it rains there is an immediate effect of coolness and wetness. However, as the rain continues and persists for days on end, different signs emerge. Rainforests are signs of longstanding and persistent rainfall. Swamps and marshes are also signs of longstanding and persistent rainfall. Crocodiles and mudfish are present where there is a lot of persistent rain. Snakes of various types, such as anacondas are found where it has rained persistently for years.

Indeed, the presence of the anointing on someone's life for a long time creates many different effects.

As you carry on building 1000 micro churches, you will grow and persist in the anointing. The fruits of the long-term presence of the anointing will be seen in your life. When there are fruits on a tree it is a sign that the tree has existed for a long time.

When God uses you to build 1000 churches, the lingering effect of the anointing will be seen on your life. You must allow the Holy Spirit to work and bring out all these powerful characteristics of a long-standing anointing. The fruits of the Holy Spirit are the fruits of the anointing. The fruits of the Holy Spirit are the products of long-standing interaction with the Holy Spirit. Abiding in the anointing means living in the anointing for many years. Abiding in the anointing means you have operated in the anointing for a long time. Fruits are evidence of a tree that has existed for a long time.

1. Abide in the anointing and walk in love. An anointed person will walk in love. As you build 1000 micro churches, you must become more loving. Amazingly, some people seem to walk less in the love of God as they progress in the ministry.

2. Stay in the anointing and walk in joy. Moodiness is a not a sign of the anointing. A long-term sign of the presence of the Holy Spirit is joy, happiness, light-hearted exuberance and excitement. Dark moods, silence and bad attitudes are a sign that the anointing of the Spirit has not permeated your life.

3. Abide in the anointing and walk in peace. Peace is an important characteristic. There are some people who increase in their contentious tendencies, as they grow older. Indeed, you should be more peaceful as you become more anointed. As you grow in the anointing, you will build 1000 micro churches. As you build 1000 micro churches, the anointing lingers on your life and there will be fewer quarrels and less contention around you. Peace is indeed a sign of the presence of the Holy Spirit.

4. Abide in the anointing and walk in forbearance. Patience, self-control and self-restraint are sure signs of a longstanding anointing. The presence of God on your life

will cause you to become patient. You will have the ability to wait for God to answer your prayers. You will have the grace to wait for God's judgment to appear in a situation. You will have the grace of God on your life to walk in self-control and in self-restraint.

5. Abide in the anointing and walk in kindness. When the anointing has been on your life for some time, you become a kind person. Kindness is a fruit of the spirit. Many people are wicked because they do not have the Holy Spirit working on their life for a long time. When a person has experienced something hurtful and does the same to others, it reveals a wicked streak. A kind-hearted person would not want others to go through the pain that they have experienced.

6. Stay in the anointing and walk in goodness. Being a good person and doing good is a sign of the longstanding presence of the Holy Spirit. How do you know there is goodness is in you? Perhaps, the less evil you emit, the more goodness has taken over your life. There is good and evil in every human being. Even the most evil people possess some goodness. When the Holy Spirit stays in your life for a long time, the goodness of God overwhelms and overrides every evil tendency and trait in your life.

7. Stay in the anointing and walk in faithfulness. Faithfulness and loyalty are signs of the presence of the Holy Spirit. Faithfulness is the same as loyalty. You may have graduated from Bible school and have a certificate in hand. You may even have the gifts of the Spirit, be able to speak in tongues and minister the word of God but still be lacking in faithfulness. Many young and immature ministers live and walk in unfaithfulness, disloyalty and treachery without thinking twice about it. As the Holy Spirit lingers and abides in their lives, characteristics like faithfulness, constancy, loyalty, trustworthiness, dependability and devotion will grow in them. Abide in the anointing and you will see these characteristics sprouting everywhere.

8. Abide in the anointing and walk in gentleness. Gentleness is a sign of the long-standing presence of the Holy Spirit. The more you are under the influence of the Holy Spirit, the gentler you will be. You will patiently and gently ease people into the will of God. Through gentleness God will accomplish greater things in your life than any amount of force and aggression can.

9. Abide in the anointing and walk in self-control. The inability to control your flesh, your moods and your attitudes are a sign that the anointing has not been with you for long. You must allow the Holy Spirit to remain in your life for a long time. Gaining control over various habits, temperaments, lifestyles, vices and evil tendencies is a sign that the Holy Spirit has lingered in your life for many years.

CHAPTER 15

Do Not Catch the Contagious Nature of Satan: Build 1000 Micro Churches

From that time on Jesus began to explain to his disciples that he must go to Jerusalem and suffer many things at the hands of the elders, the chief priests and the teachers of the law, and that he must be killed and on the third day be raised to life. Peter took him aside and began to rebuke him. "Never, Lord!" he said. "This shall never happen to you!" JESUS TURNED AND SAID TO PETER, "GET BEHIND ME, SATAN! YOU ARE A STUMBLING BLOCK TO ME; YOU DO NOT HAVE IN MIND THE CONCERNS OF GOD, BUT MERELY HUMAN CONCERNS."

Matthew 16:21-23 (NIV)

Peter caught the contagious nature of satan. This contagious nature can be picked up unintentional-ly and unknowingly. Like a spreading virus, this devilish nature can pass onto you. Sin and death have passed onto all men. It is important to reject this satanic nature as it spreads onto all men.

Therefore, just as sin entered the world through one man, and death through sin, and in this way death came to all people, because all sinned.

Romans 5:12 (NIV)

It is more natural for a human being to be a liar, a thief and immoral, than the other way round. The nature of satan has introduced sin and death to all men. The nature of satan will pass on to anyone who allows it. The nature of satan passes on to you by the invisible processes of contact and association. As you associate with rebellious people, their ideas, feelings and attitudes will rub on you. Peter imbibed the nature of satan and Jesus confronted it openly. Jesus actually called Peter, "satan".

All through the Bible, we learn that we can allow certain characteristics to grow on us or we can reject them and put on a new nature. It is very important for every Christian to be able to detect or know about the nature of satan. One of the characteristics of a severely mentally deficient child is his inability to point at things. The child does not recognize things and does not point at things. When a Christian cannot point at something and identify it as the nature of satan, he is severely spiritually deficient.

As you walk along and live on this earth, you are likely to pick up many of the traits of satan. When human beings carry on naturally, without any restraints whatsoever, they soon resemble the devil.

In your quest to build the church, you will either catch the anointing or catch the contagious nature of satan. Even though Peter became a top disciple involved in building thousands of churches, satan's nature of disobedience, pride and rebellion entered him and he began to rebuke and resist his master.

Jesus had to address the satanic nature when it arose in Peter. Do not think that because you are building the church, satan's contagious nature will not arise in you.

Monkeys differ from human beings in that they cannot point at things. They do not have the ability to notice things, to identify them and to teach others. Spiritually daft people do not have the ability to notice things, to identify them and to teach others. When satanic tendencies arise in them, they do not even know what is happening to them. They cannot identify satanic tendencies because they are not spiritually alert.

It is important to be fully aware of satanic tendencies because no one at any level is safe from these evils. Watch out for these evils and make sure you do everything to prevent them from rising up in your life. These things will prevent you from fulfilling the vision of 1000 micro churches. Do you know why many people do not accomplish the vision of 1000 micro churches? It is because they take on the traits of satan.

1. The Contagious Nature of Satan: The tendency to be lifted up in pride.

THINE HEART WAS LIFTED UP because of thy beauty, thou hast corrupted thy wisdom by reason of thy brightness: I will cast thee to the ground, I will lay thee before kings, that they may behold thee.

Ezekiel 28:17

Satan's basic nature is to be lifted up in pride. As you serve the Lord, your beauty and your wisdom will increase. This is where you must watch out. "Thou has corrupted thy wisdom by reason of thy brightness. Thine heart was lifted up. I will lay thee before kings so that they will behold thee." This is exactly what happens to proud people.

You cannot be advised when you are proud because your heart is lifted up. God wants to make you a great man of God with 1000 micro churches. Is it going to destroy you?

The lofty looks of man shall be humbled, and the haughtiness of men shall be bowed down, and the LORD alone shall be exalted in that day... And the loftiness of man shall be bowed down, and the haughtiness of men shall be made low: and the LORD alone shall be exalted in that day.

Isaiah 2:11, 17

Anything you are good at should not cause your heart to be lifted up. When your heart is lifted up, we can no longer talk to you. You can no longer be taught anything when you are proud. God wants to make you beautiful and anointed but that should not make you too big. Be careful of the tests that beauty, success, riches, knowledge and position bring.

2. The Contagious Nature of Satan: The tendency to be corrupted.

Your heart became proud on account of your beauty, and YOU CORRUPTED YOUR WISDOM because of your splendor. So I threw you to the earth; I made a spectacle of you before kings.

Ezekiel 28:17 (NIV)

As you minister the word of God, you become brighter and brighter. The tendency to allow your ministry to change you or corrupt you is real. Lucifer had a real ministry that was beautiful to behold. He was in Eden and he was precious. Preciousness can destroy a person. Being in a special place and having many privileges can corrupt you.

You were in Eden, the garden of God; every precious stone adorned you: carnelian, chrysolite and emerald, topaz, onyx and jasper, lapis lazuli, turquoise and beryl. Your settings and mountings were made of gold; on the day you were created they were prepared.

Ezekiel 28:13 (NIV)

3. The Contagious Nature of Satan: The tendency to move out of your God-given position.

> You said in your heart, "I will ascend to the heavens; I will raise my throne above the stars of God; I will sit enthroned on the mount of assembly, on the utmost heights of Mount Zaphon."
>
> Isaiah 14:13 (NIV)

Pride can make you move out of your God-given place. Lucifer wanted to ascend into heaven. Even though Lucifer was highly exalted, he wanted to move higher and deeper into places he was not permitted to go. You must be able to know and understand the restrictions God has placed on you. God has given you something but He has not given you everything. There must be order and there must be respect. There are lines you must not cross. You must not aim for things that are not yours.

4. The Contagious Nature of Satan: The tendency to cut down the high-ranking.

> You said in your heart, "I will ascend to the heavens; I will raise my throne above the stars of God; I will sit enthroned on the mount of assembly, on the utmost heights of Mount Zaphon."
>
> Isaiah 14:13 (NIV)

It is the nature of satan to desire to replace your boss. Desiring to replace your boss is different from desiring to catch the grace and anointing on somebody's life. It is the nature of satan to dislike ranks and to seek to remove differences between ranks. Certain revolutions seek to eliminate anything of a high rank. Such revolutions seek to kill kings and people of authority.

However, God Himself made us all different. It is the nature of satan to seek to equalize all things and all men. Satan seeks to cut down every big tree so that there is nothing tall or big on the landscape. Satan seeks to make everything as low as the grass, without any big trees.

Why do you hate the rich and the powerful? Why do you hate that which is beautiful and exalted? Why are you so filled with hatred and envy? It is the contagious nature of satan that has filled you with these evil tendencies.

5. The Contagious Nature of Satan: The tendency to be discontented.

Thou art the anointed cherub that covereth; and I have set thee so: thou wast upon the holy mountain of God; thou hast walked up and down in the midst of the stones of fire.

Ezekiel 28:14

It is the nature of satan to be dissatisfied and discontented with everything. People who have the contagious nature of satan are constantly complaining about things which others see as opportunities and blessings.

Was it not enough for satan to be an anointed cherub with all the coverings? Beware of people who are under you but are not satisfied with what you give them. Do not constantly be discontented, disgruntled, disaffected and dissatisfied with everything. The Israelites were filled with this terrible moral blemish. They constantly murmured against God in spite of all the great miracles He did for them.

6. The Contagious Nature of Satan: The tendency to tell lies.

Ye are of your father the devil, and the lusts of your father ye will do. He was a murderer from the beginning, and abode not in the truth, because there is no truth in him. When he speaketh a lie, he speaketh of his own: for HE IS A LIAR, AND THE FATHER OF IT.

John 8:44

Lying and deception are characteristics of the devil. Every person who is filled with deceit is affected by a demon. You must notice the presence of the devil by noticing the presence of lying and deception.

7. The Contagious Nature of Satan: The tendency to be ungrateful.

Thou art the anointed cherub that covereth; and I have set thee so: thou wast upon the holy mountain of God; thou hast walked up and down in the midst of the stones of fire.

Ezekiel 28:14

Even though Lucifer had many great experiences such as walking up and down the mountain of God, he was filled with ingratitude. Ungratefulness is a satanic trait. The world is filled with seven billion discontented people, most of whom are not grateful to God for all He has done for them. As satan's nature spreads throughout the world, ungratefulness becomes the order of the day. In the last days men shall be unthankful! (2 Timothy 3:1-2)

8. The Contagious Nature of Satan: The tendency to be forgetful.

Thou art the anointed cherub that covereth; and I HAVE SET THEE SO: thou wast upon the holy mountain of God; thou hast walked up and down in the midst of the stones of fire.

Ezekiel 28:14

God had to remind satan that it was He who had created him and put him in his position. Satan's nature is to forget the great things that have been done for you.

9. The Contagious Nature of Satan: The tendency to not be a proper part of anything.

Again there was a day when the sons of God came to present themselves before the LORD, and Satan came also among them to present himself before the LORD.

Job 2:1

Although satan was at the meeting where the sons of God presented themselves before the Lord, he was obviously not a proper part of the meeting.

Do not catch satan's contagious nature of not being fully a part of a meeting even though you are in the meeting.

Judas was a part of the disciples but his heart was not there. Part of the nature of satan is to be present fully but have a different heart.

CHAPTER 16

Do Not become a Judas: Build 1000 Micro Churches

Men and brethren, this scripture must needs have been fulfilled, which the Holy Ghost by the mouth of David spake before concerning Judas, which was guide to them that took Jesus. For he was numbered with us, and had obtained part of this ministry. Now this man purchased a field with the reward of iniquity; and falling headlong, he burst asunder in the midst, and all his bowels gushed out. And it was known unto all the dwellers at Jerusalem; insomuch as that field is called in their proper tongue, Aceldama, that is to say, The field of blood. For it is written in the book of Psalms, Let his habitation be desolate, and let no man dwell therein: and his bishoprick let another take.

Acts 1:16-20

T o build 1000 micro churches, you will need to stay around long enough. Those who drop out half way never see the glory of 1000 micro churches.

Judas is famous for rising high in the ministry and crashing out just before the finishing line. Ju-das was among the twelve original disciples. Judas had special credentials which you and I do not have. If he became the traitor we all know and detest, then all of us must be careful that we do not fall into the same trap.

Every pastor and church will experience a Judas. If Christ Himself chose people and still had a Judas, every church WILL have a Judas. You are not better than Christ.

Judases bring necessary lessons into a minister's or church's life. Judas has to come! Certain things cannot happen except there is a Judas.

Woe unto the world because of offences! for it must needs be that offences come; but woe to that man by whom the offence cometh!

Matthew 18:7

It must needs be that offences come. Judas is a great offence! But woe to the man by whom the offence cometh.

Judas mysteriously causes the will of God to come to pass. Pray that YOU will not be the Judas. Determine and decide that you will not become the Judas.

You will not be the drop-out!

The Credentials of Judas

1. Judas Iscariot was one of the original 12 disciples! You and I will never be among the original twelve disciples. If someone who was part of the first twelve people to know Christ became a traitor, what hope do you and I have who are not part of the first ten thousand disciples of Christ? Beware that you do not ever become Judas.

2. Judas was chosen by Christ Himself! If Christ, who does not make mistakes chose Judas, then I who have been chosen by a human bishop should really watch out.

3. Judas had the best training ever! If someone who had the very best training turned into a traitor, then what is your hope for remaining loyal?

4. Judas had the best teachings ever! If someone who had the very best teachings turned into a traitor, then what is your hope for remaining loyal?

5. Judas saw the best miracles ever! If someone who had the very best teachings and miracle experiences turned into a traitor, then what is your hope for remaining loyal? Even after the most amazing miracles Judas still become Judas.

6. Judas was very close to Jesus and yet he became a traitor. Judas' closeness to Christ did not prevent him from turning into a traitor. Everyone who is close must take note of this warning. Being close is not a guarantee that you will not become Judas. In fact, you will have to be a close person to become Judas.

7. Judas was a personal friend of Christ. The devil has no new tricks only variations of the same theme. He will work out the same trick and he always has some people who fall for the trick. Decide not to be one who will fall for this trick of being turned from a longstanding, close and personal friend into a traitor.

8. Judas had many meals with Christ and still became a traitor. Many of us have not even had a meal with our pastor, let alone the bishop of the church. Being so close as to eat and share food with your leader does not mean that you cannot become a treacherous traitor.

9. Judas was appointed to a very high up and sensitive position in the church and still became a traitor. Judas was the accountant. The accountant in the church knows everything. Judas knew many things and yet this knowledge did not protect him from becoming a traitor.

10. Judas Iscariot saw much more than we have seen but he still became 'Judas'. God never does things just to impress people. The most powerful miracles were done before a few people. Judas saw every single miracle.

11. Judas was under the best kind of leadership and yet he became a traitor. Please note that very good leaders do have traitors. The fact that someone has treacherous people in his team does not mean that he has done something wrong.

How to Prevent Yourself from Becoming Judas

1. Do not be offended if you are the odd-one-out.

Judas was not from Galilee. Everybody else was from Galilee. Judas was from Cherioth.

An odd-one-out is exposed to many more temptations to become a traitor. Odd-ones-out are exposed to more evil thoughts and temptations. An odd-one-out is prone to offence. An odd-one-out will be hurt at the slightest instance.

What is an odd-one-out? An odd-one-out can be any of these things. Watch out for offence if you fall into any of these categories!

1. You are odd when you are a woman amongst many men.

2. You are an odd-one-out when you are uneducated and live amongst educated people.

3. You are an odd-one-out when everybody is married and you are not married.

4. You are an odd-one-out when everybody has a child and you don't have a child.

5. You are an odd-one-out when everybody has a car and you don't have a car.

6. You are an odd-one-out when everybody comes from a particular country and you are from a different country.

7. You are an odd-one-out when everyone comes from a particular tribe and culture except you.

8. You are an odd-one-out when everybody passed an exam but you didn't.

9. You are an odd-one-out when everybody's church is growing but yours is not.

10. You are an odd-one-out when everybody is travelling but you are not travelling.

11. You are an odd-one-out when everybody has a nice house but you don't have a nice house.

12. You are an odd-one-out when everybody chats with the pastor but you cannot find anything to say to him.

13. You are an odd-one-out when everybody has a "beloved" but you don't have one.

14. You are an odd-one-out when everybody has a decent job but you are always given the 'dirty' work.

15. You are an odd-one-out when everybody is being sent to a nice place but not you.

16. You are an odd-one-out when everyone is in a relationship but you have broken up yours.

17. You are an odd-one-out when everybody has been appointed as a pastor but you were not appointed.

18. You are an odd-one-out when everybody was invited to the party but you were not.

19. You are an odd-one-out when everyone is a white man but you are the only black person.

20. You are an odd-one-out when everyone is a black man but you are the only white person.

2. Do not be offended.

Judas was an usher. Judas was a waiter in the church. Judas was an errand boy. Judas was a scavenger. Judas could have been offended at these menial tasks.

And Jesus said, Make the men sit down. Now there was much grass in the place. So the men sat down, in number about five thousand. And Jesus took the loaves; and when he had given thanks, he distributed to the disciples, and the disciples to them that were set down; and likewise of the fishes as much as they would.

John 6:10-11

3. Do not be deceived by familiarity.

Yea, mine own familiar friend, in whom I trusted, which did eat of my bread, hath lifted up his heel against me.

Psalm 41:9

"My own familiar friend ...hath lifted up his heel against me." When you are too familiar with somebody you only see his ordinariness. You forget he is also anointed. Gradually, you begin to despise him. That is why kings and chiefs do not eat in public. We are more able to receive Jesus now than the people of His day. I once heard someone describing the senior pastors of the land as "expired fathers". Don't think your father has become weaker because he is speaking about love and humility. Judas probably misinterpreted the message on the burden of love. People think that love is weak. But love is strong! Love is as strong as death! (Song of Solomon 8:6)

CHAPTER 17

Do Not become a Drop-Out: Build 1000 Micro Churches

Ye did run well; who did hinder you that ye should not obey the truth?

Galatians 5:7

It is important that you do not drop out of the ministry. What is the point of running well and crashing out at the last minute? All through the Bible we see many examples of people who ran well and crashed out at the last minute.

If you crash out of the ministry, a thousand churches that should have come out from you will be lost. God wants to use you! Failure is not an option! You will bring forth 1000 micro churches!

Top Seven Drop-Outs

1. **JUDAS:** Judas dropped out of the ministry of Jesus Christ. He is the most famous of all ministry drop-outs. Make sure you do not end up like Judas. Judas had the best of everything and yet he fell out of the greatest team and he fell away from the greatest leader.

   Men and brethren, this scripture must needs have been fulfilled, which the Holy Ghost by the mouth of David spake before concerning JUDAS, WHICH WAS GUIDE TO THEM THAT TOOK JESUS. FOR HE WAS NUMBERED WITH US, and had obtained part of this ministry. Now this man purchased a field with the reward of iniquity; and falling head-long, he burst asunder in the midst, and all his bowels gushed out.

   Acts 1:16-18

2. **DEMAS:** Demas is well known for forsaking apostle Paul. Demas' problem was that he loved the world. Demas was one of the brethren who would send salutations and greeting with Apostle Paul. He was an integral part of the ministry. At the end of Paul's life, where he wrote, "I have finished my course" we read that Demas had forsaken Paul. Make sure you do not end up like Demas.

   Epaphras, who is one of you, a servant of Christ, saluteth you, always labouring fervently for you in prayers, that ye may stand perfect and complete in all the will of God. For I bear him record, that he hath a great zeal for you, and them that are in Laodicea, and them in Hierapolis. Luke, the beloved physician, and DEMAS, GREET YOU.

Colossians 4:12-14

There salute thee Epaphras, my fellowprisoner in Christ Jesus; Marcus, Aristarchus, DEMAS, Lucas, my fellowlabourers.

Philemon 1:23-24

For I am now ready to be offered, and THE TIME OF MY DEPARTURE IS AT HAND. I have fought a good fight, I HAVE FINISHED MY COURSE, I have kept the faith: Henceforth there is laid up for me a crown of righteousness, which the Lord, the righteous judge, shall give me at that day: and not to me only, but unto all them also that love his ap-pearing. Do thy diligence to come shortly unto me: FOR DEMAS HATH FORSAKEN ME, having loved this present world, and is departed unto Thessalonica; Crescens to Gala-tia, Titus unto Dalmatia.

2 Timothy 4:6-10

3. **JOHN MARK:** John Mark is well-known for forsaking Apostle Paul in the ministry. He was a sore point of contention between Paul and Barnabas. Paul did not want to continue working with a renegade pastor like John Mark but Barnabas had a different opinion. Make sure you do not end up like John Mark.

Now when Paul and his company loosed from Paphos, they came to Perga in Pamphylia: and John departing from them returned to Jerusalem.

Acts 13:13

And Barnabas determined to take with them John, whose surname was Mark. But Paul thought not good to take him with them, who departed from them from Pamphylia, and went not with them to the work.

Acts 15:37-38

Only Luke is with me. Take Mark, and bring him with thee: for he is profitable to me for the ministry.

2 Timothy 4:11

4. **HYMENAEUS AND ALEXANDER:** Hymenaeus and Alexander are famous for having made a disaster of the ministry. They were so far gone that Paul had to deliver them to satan so that they would learn not to blaspheme. Make sure you do not ever get to the place where you need to be handed over to satan himself.

Holding faith, and a good conscience; which some having put away concerning faith have made shipwreck: Of whom is Hymenaeus and Alexander; whom I have delivered unto Satan, that they may learn not to blaspheme.

1 Timothy 1:19-20

5. **GEHAZI:** Gehazi is famous for not catching the anointing and falling out of the ministry of Elisha. Whereas Elisha caught the anointing that was on Elijah, Gehazi received a curse and became a leper. He crashed out of the stream of anointing that had been flowing since the days of Elijah. Make sure you do not walk in the ways of Gehazi and crash out of a beautiful stream of the anointing.

But he went in, and stood before his master. And Elisha said unto him, Whence comest thou, Gehazi? And he said, Thy servant went no whither. And he said unto him, Went not mine heart with thee, when the man turned again from his chariot to meet thee? Is it a time to receive money, and to receive garments, and oliveyards, and vineyards, and sheep, and oxen, and menservants, and maidservants? The leprosy therefore of Naaman shall cleave unto thee, and unto thy seed for ever. And he went out from his presence a leper as white as snow.

2 Kings 5:25-27

6. **NADAB AND ABIHU:** These sons of Aaron are famous for being destroyed in the midst of their ministry. They offered strange fire to the Lord and they died before the

Lord in the midst of their years. Instead of completing the great calling to priesthood, they were destroyed for doing the wrong things in the ministry.

And Nadab and Abihu, the sons of Aaron, took either of them his censer, and put fire therein, and put incense thereon, and offered strange fire before the LORD, which he commanded them not. And there went out fire from the LORD, and devoured them, and they died before the LORD.

Leviticus 10:1-2

7. **MANY UNNAMED DISCIPLES:** Many unnamed disciples did not make it to the end of the ministry. They dropped out when they heard a hard message from Jesus Christ. As you can see, being a drop-out is not as rare as it seems. Many unnamed disciples became drop-outs. Make sure you are not among the unnamed disciples who amount to nothing in God and in the ministry.

And he said, therefore said I unto you, that no man can come unto me, except it were given unto him of my Father. From that time MANY OF HIS DISCIPLES WENT BACK, AND WALKED NO MORE WITH HIM. Then said Jesus unto the twelve, Will ye also go away?"

John 6:65-67

Conclusion

It is my prayer that you will rise up and build 1000 micro churches. Do not drop out of the race! Do not receive the contagious nature of satan! Believe that you will become a nation! Believe that a little one will become a thousand! I see 1000 micro churches coming out of you!

To the making of many books there is no end!

BV - #0001 - 140422 - C0 - 212/135/7 - PB - 9600690000093 - Gloss Lamination